YELLOWLEGS

YELLOWLEGS

John Janovy, Jr.

ST. MARTIN'S PRESS   New York

Designed by Mina Grienstien

Library of Congress Cataloging in Publication Data

Janovy, John, Jr.
  Yellowlegs.

  1. Lesser yellowlegs. I. Title.
QI696.C48J36   598'.33   80-15947
ISBN 0-312-89643-3

Lyrics on page 183 from "Y'all Come Back Saloon"
by Sharon Vaughn, copyright © 1977 Jack and
Bill Music Company, % Welk Music Group, Santa
Monica, CA 90401. International copyright secured.
All rights reserved. Used by permission.

*To those who seek their futures
among the wild*

Contents

Part III ⌒
SPRING

Acknowledgments

T here are always other people who help—some directly, some indirectly, many without knowing it—in the preparation of a manuscript. I would like to thank those who have made such a contribution, but I need to specifically mention those of whose help I am aware. Jim Dvorak and Anne Schuster, thanks for the coffee and conversation once a week; you provided an outlet for some mighty different kinds of thoughts during the writing of this book. Dick Boohar, thanks for your editorial help on the early versions of this thing, although I'm sure you know you were well paid. When I gave you that kingfisher painting in exchange for your services, there was a bit of my soul attached to the back. Pam Rhoten (Eldridge), thanks for all that typing. For those of you who think university professors have a lot of good sense, consider the fact that I turned my whole office over to an eighteen-year-old girl a few years ago and told her to take care of my professional life for a thousand dollars a year. And if you don't believe a lot of unbelievable things happen at a university, consider the fact that it worked. Thanks, Pam, for keeping my desk clean, your typewriter busy, and my professional life organized. Well, the bit with the freshman girl worked out so well that I tried it again, and I do sincerely thank you, Monica Murtaugh, for coming along to keep my desk clean, your typewriter busy, and my professional life organized. I should have had some mercy, I suppose, but then what better way to learn what you've gotten yourself into than to take this latest scribbled *Yellowlegs* draft off to your dorm room to type! Paul Johnsgard, a writer of prodigious productivity and uncompromising dedication to the wild things of this planet, thanks for reading this manuscript and for the benefits of your ornithological comments.

My deepest appreciation must be expressed to Dr. G. M. Sutton, one of my former teachers who opened up his library to me one spring day in 1979 and who had the patience to read through an early version of this story. In that library I discovered an incredible fact: there was a time in history when the overland/overocean speed record for long-distance flights of migrating birds was held by the lesser yellowlegs. Nineteen hundred and thirty miles in five days, that was the record then. From that publication in Dr. Sutton's library, I learned the band number of that bird. Before this story is over, you will understand completely the significance of that discovery in the library last spring.

Finally, there is a former teacher of mine, a man who is still my teacher, Dr. J. T. Self. There was a time back in the 1960s when he sent me out after yellowlegs, to Kansas, to the Gulf Coast, yes, even to Rockport, and it has come as a surprise even to me that the memories of that chase have lingered so long and so strongly that they may be found throughout this manuscript. In fact, those memories may be the very things ultimately responsible for the generation of this manuscript. Follow the yellowlegs! What an impossible and mind-boggling task! But he sent me out to do it one time almost twenty years ago. I learned some things about America then, Dr. Self, that can finally be told. They're in the pages that follow.

JOHN JANOVY, JR.
September 1979

10

Part I
THE ECOLOGIST

1 ⌒ The Prairies

Its spell is on me like a brand,
It has marked me for its own.

Kenneth Kaufman
Level Land

O ne of these days I'm going to leave Nebraska, cut all those strings and ties and travel to the other prairies of this earth. I must know if the people who live on those other prairies feel the same way about their horizons as we do about ours. I must know if there are places where cottonwood-like trees grow, where migrating sandpipers gather, where the braided rivers course, and where humans get that strangled-up feeling unless they can see eight or ten miles across grass.

If you've been here in the winter, you know how those dark clouds come roiling in over the grain elevators out west of town, spitting sleet, leaving a glaze over everything. If you've read about us in the spring, you know about those late snows that hit at calving time, and you know about ranchers who kick into a drift to find the first frozen muzzle of fifty newborn calves down under there somewhere. If you've driven through here in mid-summer, maybe on your way to Colorado, then you know of the killing heat of the prairies, you've smelled the pungent green haze of alfalfa drying, and you've seen sunburned boys around a combine in a cloud of wheat dust. But if you've lived here all your life, you've seen those clouds of waterfowl come in low over the cottonwoods, you know

13

there are times when sandhill cranes fill the morning chill with the most primeval calls of all the earth, and you know there are times when sandpipers gather around waters' edges. If you've lived here all your life, then you certainly know that at those places where the sandpipers gather, you'll find a certain bird. And if things haven't gone quite right today, you'll find me there, too, off in the weeds, binoculars propped up in the mud, simply watching some yellow-shanked sandpiper, wondering with all my heart and mind whether I should once again fly with that animal to the ends of the earth.

It's at the end of the summer when these feelings come most strongly. There is something about the end of summer that produces all sorts of strange yearnings in people like me. Maybe it's the cooling weather. I don't really think it's fair that fall should start in the middle of August, and I think it's even less fair that *school* should start in August. All the good things that humanity has accomplished out here on the prairies show that the plains people are capable of many amazing feats, but why this decision to begin school during the month of August, I'll never know. It almost seems the final insult to a sandpiper mind. At a time when we should be going, some authority says we should be staying. I think there must be many ways to learn about the world, many things to see outside a classroom in August or even in September. There must be thousands of kinds of insects, little fishes, worms, out there on the mudflats where the yellowlegs gather, and so why, I keep asking myself, why couldn't that also be a place where schoolboys gather?

Maybe the movements of all those animals could teach a kid as much as some older person in a hot classroom, pages from *National Geographic* stapled up around on all the bulletin boards, desks smelling of varnish, and the sounds of grasshoppers drifting in open windows along with the laughter of recess. Yes, I believe that a person could learn every bit as much about the world we live in by stomping through the mud after yellowlegs and little things in the water as by sitting in some classroom or some office or some committee meeting or over some set of ledgers or reports. I can also tell you now from a great deal of personal experience that the world of August schoolrooms and city business may not be ready for that kind of education. And I can tell you now from that same set of personal experiences that stomping through the mud after sandpipers in August is sure to launch you into a migration of the mind from which you may never return to what we often call "civilization."

It begins to rain again out here on the prairies in late August, early September, and the water accumulates in standing puddles, sometimes several acres in size, off in the corners of wheat stubble. You can see teal out in those puddles and killdeer along the edges, but most of all you can see real sandpipers. Their long wings cut that prairie air in a way no blackbird's could ever do, their legs trail total grace, and they sometimes twist and turn, calling their soft but insistent calls as they set gliding into that rain puddle off in the corner of some field. How many times as a kid I stood off in the sunflowers along a fence row, sticky in the afternoon heat, and watched those sandpipers around a rain puddle, wondering, just wondering, from where they came and where they were going, how they made their way in this world where semis roared out on the interstate. How many times as a kid I turned back toward home late in the afternoon, the flights of yellowlegs seared in emotional images into the back of my brain, knowing that the very next day I would be sitting in that stifling classroom next to some junior-high girl who could either run faster than I or make me feel like an embarrassed idiot, depending on how her hormones flowed that morning.

Those years are long past now, as are the years I spent as an adult remembering what it was like to be a kid dreaming of flying with those sandpipers. There is no doubt in my mind now that to follow a sandpiper is to learn things in a way that no teacher, no classroom, no public school, and especially no university could ever teach! For now, now as an adult with all the responsibilities most adults have, sitting at my typewriter as once again August turns to fall, as once again school's obscene beginning looms amidst the quiet of Indian Summer, as once again the yellowlegs gather around those puddles I know are out west of here, I have the knowledge that about this time last year I said to hell with it all and followed that yellow-shanked bird through what I call The Tropics to the end of the earth.

These prairies start somewhere up in Canada, up where the yellowlegs nest, up where those incredibly beautiful and delicate sandpiper chicks are thrust out into the wilderness. These prairies roll southward down through what we call the Dakotas. Harsh lands, the Dakotas, given over to sturdy people, tough people, rodeo cowboys, the colors of yellow and brown, and in the spring and fall, those migrating birds. These prairies roll southward into my beloved Sandhills, twenty thousand square miles of dunes, hard grass, the most fiercely independent cussed ranchers you ever met, wet sloughs and prairie marshes where larvae squirm their hours in the vile mud before some weary yellowlegs snaps them up to fuel a several-thousand-mile flight to Argentina, and who knows, maybe beyond. These prairies run southward into Kansas, that fairest and most fertile of prairie states, with oil and gas beneath those Flint Hills and waves of bluestem. Kansas has always been my favorite prairie state and for some very good reasons. I began this life as a follower of animals while standing in a Kansas marsh. I may have this higher degree from a place in Oklahoma, but my *real* education began years and years ago in the middle of Kansas in the middle of a cloud of mosquitoes, in the middle of a marsh, with sandpipers on the horizon. And Oklahoma—who could ever forget Oklahoma, rampant, laid-back, untamed, blood-red Oklahoma, where welfare is a major industry, oil is a major industry, college football is a major industry, and amidst the wonder of it all lies a single pond where I once almost touched a living, wild yellowlegs. And Texas. There is an electricity to the atmosphere of Texas. You can feel that charge the moment you cross the Red River. Dallas and Houston are modern, and there is much money, very much money, in the state of Texas. There is also a small town on the Gulf of Mexico, and the sandpipers gather at this small town of Rockport in the spring and fall. Of all my memories of Texas, that day in Rockport stands clearly as one of the turning points of my life. I will simply never forget that old woman nor that lesson in technology I received at the hands of Mother Nature that day in Rockport.

The pioneers who first came to the prairies called them the Great

American Desert, and only the most brazen stayed here to try and bend the will of the grasslands to serve human needs. Resourceful, above all a person needs to be resourceful to survive out here. And self-reliant, a person needs to be self-reliant to survive the isolation of the prairies, to envision the lonely migrations of those creatures that pass along the clouds in the distance. Ingenious, it helps to be ingenious if you're going to try to live out here for very long. Now that we've entered the modern machine age, I see the results of a century or more of prairie resourcefulness, self-reliance, and ingenuity, and sometimes it breaks my heart. The problem is water or rather the fact that there is not much of it.

Everywhere I look out across my prairies I see modern technology applied to the problem of water. There are machines called "center pivot sprinklers," but you should just accept the fact that I don't have the literary skill to describe to you a center pivot sprinkler. You just have to see one, or better yet, stand beneath one. From the air, center pivots remind me of virus particles as seen through an electron microscope. There are places in Nebraska where you can turn a small plane away from the sands of the Platte River, head out over the center pivots, and look down onto one of the most symmetrical, organized patterns of circles you ever saw. I think that center pivots are the kinds of things some visitors from outer space would see and use as evidence for habitation of this planet. To me, however, they look like virus particles in an electron micrograph of an infected cell. In my private moments, I draw an analogy between infected cells and an infected prairie: the center pivots are sucking us dry, sapping the very lifeblood of the prairie, the water below the land.

And the Platte River—that mighty river of sand and ring-billed gulls—has been manipulated, dammed, diverted, as have the two rivers that converge to form the Platte: the South Platte, snaking out from the mountains west of Denver and trickling out across the prairies; and the North Platte, bending back on itself through the Medicine Bow range in Wyoming. Every drop, it seems, in those rivers has been the subject of debate in my state's legislature, has been the subject of discussion among those who live along the rivers, has been fought over, chased, captured, sent out to irrigate a corn field, or with a begrudging eye watched pass over the state line

17

at Omaha. I am totally convinced that if we had our way, Iowa and Missouri would never see a single drop of Platte water! I am totally convinced that if Colorady had *its* way, we wouldn't see it either! Ecological soapboxes aside, however, one must admire the gall of generations of engineers who have viewed these prairie rivers as nothing more than things to manipulate. They have turned our rivers into toys, giant toys, laid out across the land, and they play with these toys continually in the name of water.

There are great stretches of sand in those rivers. "Braided" is the word to describe these rivers, for from the air they do indeed look braided, with twisting narrow channels and twisting twining sandbars, their waters nourishing the cottonwoods with leaves gently clattering in the fall breeze. To me, however, these rivers don't mean "water," they mean "sandpipers." No matter how much the engineers try to manipulate my rivers through dams and diversions, parts of these rivers seem to remain wild. Maybe it's only my mind that remains wild, maybe it's only my mind that's able to bend reality to see the wilderness in a prairie river that has been so manipulated by modern irrigation technology, but I don't think so. There are places on the prairie where the rivers have been "tamed," put to work to supply the vegetative needs of a local human population. But downstream from those places the river is wild again. Or at least the river seems wild. Sandpipers walk the wet sands, and most of these days a single sandpiper spells "wilderness" to me.

But the true wilderness is to be found in the moving sands of those rivers. There is an awesome evolutionary power in the movements of those sands, for those movements are the same ones that erase mountain ranges and level continents. Even the weakest of humans can stand in that prairie river and feel the moving sand around his ankles. It almost seems as if the river is excusing itself from human company, gently moving that sand from beneath human feet. That kind of feeling can make you feel small in a hurry, and that kind of feeling, especially when you have your binocs trained on a yellowlegged sandpiper at the same time, can make you feel like an intruder. "Excuse me," you want to say to the living river, "for having stepped on your sands, sullied your waters and seen your private yellowlegs."

18

"That's all right!" the living river seems to reply, "I'll just excuse myself from your company, move my sands from beneath your feet."

But you always have this feeling that the river is toying with you, that the river has options for changing the face of the planet that maybe you don't have, so there often comes another feeling, this one almost of terrified fear, when you're standing beneath one of those high earthen dams. You can feel the river somehow still retains the option of excusing itself from human company and can use the force it has, that force which can level a continent, to throw aside a feeble human structure such as an earthen damn. You think maybe that in their naive gall, those people who tried to dam my river forty years ago never gave enough consideration to forces that are the same ones which erase mountain ranges and level continents!

I suppose this is a good time to admit that I am somewhat of an environmentalist. Amazingly enough, I still teach biology at a large university located in one of the prairie states, although I'm sure that such an act of disgusted rebellion as I displayed a year ago would have been grounds for dismissal. I am also a distinguished scientist, but I don't look like one and generally don't act like one either. I have learned some things about life on the prairies that not everyone knows, and once you've learned those things then you're a little less inclined to affect the pomp and circumstance of distinguished scientists.

Most of what I've learned in the last year concerns the natural history of a sandpiper, a lesser yellowlegs. I don't need to tell most of you that the libraries are filled with books on the natural history of sandpipers, including the lesser yellowlegs. However, I'm not at all sure that there is anywhere in those libraries a book that describes the way this species of sandpiper deals with the technological state as manifest out here on the prairies. Yes, we are civilized out here on the prairies, and yes, modern technology and all its subspecies can be found out here on the prairies right alongside sandpipers. That's one of the things I learned in the last few months from studying the lesser yellowlegs. Or more properly, I should say *a* lesser yellowlegs. One of the other things I learned out here on the prairies in the last year is that the lesser yellowlegs has to face almost every minute of its life the manifestations of our technological age. We now live in the most technical society to ever have evolved within the human population on the face of this Earth, and if you think for one moment that wild things don't have to deal with that technology every instant of their lives, then you are very wrong.

Finally, if you think for one moment you can discover that aforementioned fact without *leaving* the technological state, then you are also very wrong. Maybe that's why I have trouble affecting the pomp and circumstance of a distinguished scientist. I found out about this time last year that if you're going to study an animal very seriously, then you have to leave the technological condition and begin acting like an animal. I did that about a year ago. I should have expected that the experience would take me to countries of the mind from which I might not return, since that has happened also with most of my other research projects. Seems that science has a way of taking you to new places of understanding, to new fields of truths, across oceans of ignorance to exotic islands of insight.

I suppose in some ways you could call this document a Report to the American Public of my last year's research upon the natural history of *Tringa flavipes* (Gmelin) 1789, the lesser yellowlegs. But I've read lots of reports and done lots of research upon which reports were written, and this one is like no other. In order to gather these facts I had to spend the better part of a year acting more like an animal than a human, all for the sake of my research on one gray sandpiper. Yes, the time has come to admit that there was only one bird. No, I'm not talking about one *species,* I'm talking about one *bird.* She was banded.

I'm not going to tell you the band number, for you would just track it down, and you would then know who put that band on her. You would probably write to tell me who that person was, and I don't want to know who had their hands on my bird first. At any rate, there will be times in the pages that follow when you ask, "How does that guy *know* that this actually happened to that bird? How does *he* know?" And so I will answer that question right now: I know because I have seen the yellowlegs, I have crawled in the mud with the yellowlegs, and I have followed that yellowlegs to land's end. That's how I know.

20

2 ⟶ On Leave

Going after Cacciato

Tim O'Brien

*T*here comes a time in a scientist's life when some decisions
are necessary. Leave time is one of those times. Heaven knows we
all earn and need our sabbaticals, but there are such mixed feelings
about actually *taking* the time off. Some I've known have labored
their entire professional lives—thirty, forty years without leave—
mainly because of the fear that there would be no place for them
when they returned. Others have done the same thing, worked
forty years in a row, but for different reasons. These scientists I can
sympathize with. They love their work; it is probably their life.
The only thing they could envision doing with free time is more of
what they're doing with their spare time. I think some of us may
have a fear that time will no longer be so productively spent when it
is not so dear, when it doesn't have to be carved out of an already
full day and night. But above all, leave time should be a time for
thinking, for reflection, for the adjustment of a career, for
synthesis, perhaps for pursuit of some intellectual dream that
scurries through the tall grass of the prairie minds! The lucky ones
are those with dreams and the guts to pursue them. Maybe "guts"
is the wrong word. I know in my own case that pursuit of my
childhood dream might well be attributed to lack of good sense.

I applied for my sabbatical a great many months ago, well before
I had a clear idea what I would do with the time should it be
granted. I had some vague notion that it was time to become an

ecologist, for I had toyed with that science for a number of years and had even spent my time in the environments of several prairie states. But the years had flown, and I had become victim to the reductionist philosophies that now color the atmospheres of high science. The grant money flowed into my laboratory in a gushing stream, tens and even hundreds of thousands of dollars, and I spent it all without the slightest twinge of regret or conscience, most of it pursuing those ideas which seemed to be a natural part of the technological age. All life processes, including the nesting of swallows and the migrations of sandpipers, could be explained if only we could find the right molecule, said those philosophies, and for the sake of money, pride and tenure, I agreed. The computer, man's finest machine, could quantify and explain even the wilderness of a braided river, said those philosophies, and for years I raised no possibility of an alternative explanation for that same wilderness. But a scientist who does not change, grow continuously, at least evaluate new philosophies, is a scientist who is dead. We may be living in the midst of a technological explosion the likes of which humanity has never before witnessed, but we are also living in an age in which voices cry out for the preservation of wilderness, the survival of species, and for the conservation of resources. No person who has stood as a child in the row of sticky sunflowers and watched a flock of yellowlegs come turning, calling to one another, into that rain puddle, or who has kept alive a childhood dream of flying with those birds, could ignore such voices. So when my request for sabbatical was denied, I sat at my desk with that letter in hand and said to hell with it. I would become an ecologist anyway.

You must know that this business of ours is at once both the most challenging and the most draining. It is exhausting work, spilling your brains to a sea of freshman faces three hours a week, but the rewards are many. Over the years, however, a sameness pervades, and when that happens then you know for the sake of your students that it is time for a leave. Research is the only answer, and most of us are able to forestall that creeping sameness by our research efforts. Teaching is draining, your best ideas are spent, your communication tricks are used, your tolerance and patience are distributed to all who need them, and you stand at the bus stop one afternoon as fall turns to winter and realize that you are empty. *Research! Research,* on the other hand, is filling! Those best ideas come at the most unexpected times: sitting in some grungy college-town bar, squirming on a hard pew at church, standing over a sink full of test tubes and culture plates covered with wild fungus. You write them down in excited henscratch on the nearest scrap of paper! Later you muse, refine those ideas, sitting early in the morning over coffee, shuffling through paper napkins, pledge cards, bits of junk mail, the business card of some used-car salesman, all with a Nobel Prize idea hurriedly scratched on the back in your beer-blurred writing! You rush to the laboratory and put those ideas into practice! The experiment works! You have data! Data! Data! We have data! you hear yourself saying, almost as some Houston voice might say, Lift-off! We have Lift-off! When that happens, you step out into the first blowing sleet of winter and don't feel a thing. You are filled with something. One such day sustains many days in the classroom. But even an incisive mind grows dull after a few years. The ritualistic search for money, the prostitution of your ideas for Federal money, blunts the cutting edge of creativity. Sameness creeps into your lectures and your notes scratched on bar napkins. Then it's time for sabbatical.

I mentioned money. Nasty word—money. Nice when you have it in some account, terrible when you don't. Nice when you have it to spend on chemicals, cheap glassware, bewildering when you don't. You would be surprised what money will do for your thoughts. Too little money and your thoughts are keen, economical, cunning, synthetic. You have to get the most for your money, your research dollar, so you combine your best knowledge of living things with your latest knowledge of biological technology, and the result is some of your best research. Adequate money and your work gets sloppy. You spend too much time doing research for the sole purpose of getting more money at renewal time. That is not healthy. Too much money, that is the healthiest of all conditions. Too much money and you budget a significant portion for gambling. And as we all know, it is the out-and-out gamble in pure science that produces the quantum leap in understanding, the truly new discovery. The history of science tells us that smart people budget for such a gamble regardless of the amount of money they have.

23

I can tell you that gambling with Federal money is a very difficult thing to convince yourself to do. But I do it all the time, spending some fraction of a big grant on what seems on the surface to be a stupid and farfetched idea. Most of the data pertaining to my basic, intelligent and logical scientific ideas still lie buried in my research files. Most of the observations pertaining to my farfetched ideas, my wildcats, are published in journals which require anonymous review by my peers. I have given you all this background regarding money and the history of science for one very simple reason: my sabbatical application rejected, I was without funds to support my leave, but my decision to become an ecologist was all gamble. Nothing in my library could have predicted the things I would discover about the lesser yellowlegs, the species upon which I finally concentrated. Nor would any Federal agency have funded such ill-defined research as I at first envisioned: a stroll out along the Platte River to see what I could see.

In retrospect, I see that my meagre research budget and inadequate equipment contributed the expected cunning to my work. In retrospect, this whole venture, all my resources, were gambled on the vague idea that a stroll along the Platte would make me the ecologist I thought it was time to be, would replenish my stores of understanding which my students had drained. My equipment probably needs to be mentioned first: binoculars, a white porcelain pan about eight inches wide and ten inches long, and a quarter-inch minnow seine. The most basic and simple of ecological tools! If there is any piece of scientific equipment that needs to be added to such a list, it is that *most* functional of items: a human brain. My research budget also needs mentioning. It consisted of my life savings: $1,756.88; and that includes last quarter's interest. I remember standing in that bank lobby in my field clothes, binocs slung around my neck, white pan tucked smartly underneath my left arm, seine rolled tightly on its poles thrown casually over my right shoulder, sabbatical denial letter filed carefully in my wastebasket, and withdrawing my life savings—$1,756.88. The young lady teller mentioned something about last quarter's interest. That all took place almost exactly one year ago.

A year ago! I have little recollection of the wild thoughts that must have been in my head that one year ago, standing at that counter! All is gone prior to that, too, it seems, all obliterated, all sunk into the obscurity that in lighter moments I call dates and times PY, *pre-yellowlegs!* All has been replaced by drifting images of the Platte, of creatures that stalk its shifting sands, and of course my thoughts and experiences over the last year. Those thoughts include my evaluation of one of the finest teachers I have ever known: a small-town auto mechanic whose visions of the machine age form the basis for the message of this tale. Those thoughts include my assessment of the philosophical corners we have worked ourselves into with our reductionist dependency upon convenience technology, or reverence for machinery. Maybe I should qualify that last phrase: machinery which is made of iron, steel, synthetic fabrics, copper wire, and human creative intelligence lobotomied into a servo-mechanism role. There is other machinery of this World, other machinery for which we could use a little *more* reverence: that finest of machinery is made of skin, bone, feathers, and a primeval will to fly.

And the experiences—communicated in the most direct and truthful way so you may evaluate for yourself the basic scientific observations of my last year out upon the Great Plains of North America—in abstract, those experiences include everything from a stroll along the Platte to an indescribable impasse between the machine age and the mysterious world of nature on the beach at Rockport, Texas. But always, it seems, always haunting the morning horizons of my memories, is that bird, wending its migrations through my every thought now that I have returned, weaving a tortuous path through my country, *the most technical society to have ever arisen on the face of this planet,* and finally pointing her long bill in the directions I must follow.

Well, I am still a college professor, and I still teach biology here in the midst of the Great Plains of North America. Classes begin tomorrow, and I will walk into that auditorium at eight-thirty tomorrow morning to face a sea of anxious freshmen. There will be over two hundred of them, smiling, with lingering remnants of summer tans, with scarcely hidden apprehensions about college life. There will be some who have struggled through high school but will set the world on fire. There will be some who will fail miserably at everything they do, there will be some who will lose scholarships because of bad grades, and there may be one who will be President. There will be people who never come to class but destroy my exams, and there will be some whose parents have expectations which will never be realized. There will be some from small towns and some from ghettos. They will all expect the world from me, and *tomorrow, this* year, of all years in my rambling life, they just damn well might get it! You ask, "Why?" and of course I can answer that without hesitation: I have returned refreshed; I have seen the yellowlegs, I have crawled in the mud with the yellowlegs, and I have followed that banded gray lady to land's end. That's why.

3 ᴥ The Master Mechanic

. . . oh hell, John, just drive it on in!

Glenn Oneth

My mind was on cars, I remember, when I first began my leave, and the reason was probably Glenn's recent and untimely death from a pancreatic ailment. When those close to you die, you often review their lives, ask what it is they took and what it is they left, and almost a year ago to the day I was asking those very questions. Glenn was the most earthy of men, uneducated—he'd left school very early to work upon the Model T—and thrice married, but beyond all things, he was skillful with his hands. When I first met him, he was a grizzled old bird and I was a college kid with a keen interest in his daughter. When I last saw him, he lay in his casket, symbolic grease still beneath his fingernails, and I sat in a pew and listened while some Baptist preacher called his body a "Master Mechanic." That event was fresh on my mind a year ago, and of course since Glenn's whole life had consisted of Ford Automobiles, I couldn't help thinking about those most educational of machines. I was on the outskirts of town a year ago, on my way to some ecological research along the Platte River, and my first stop was to be Grand Island. That fact, too, I suppose, was responsible for my thoughts of automobiles. It is eighty-eight miles to Grand Island across these prairies, and I was walking.

Walking is rote exercise, but when you're after some experiences with Mother Nature, then there's no substitute for it. Personally, I would much rather ride, especially if the object of my stroll is eighty-eight miles away. It was muggy that day, and before I'd gone even a few miles, I stopped for beer. Right away, that, too, reminded me of Glenn. We drank an awful lot of beer together, as well as some bourbon served cold out of a half-pint approved by a hard smack on the bottom of the little bottle. Seems there are lots of things in this world remind me of that man.

Although Glenn never took any leave, he was still one of the finest teachers I've ever known. He lived in a small town in Oklahoma, he did lots of work on cars that I owned, and he rendered a lot of opinions on cars that I wanted to buy. He used to sit on his late-summer lawn, in this red Oklahoma town which the interstate had bypassed, and watch a whole parade of cars rattle down a brick-paved street. You could tell by his eyes those were cars he'd worked on at one time or another. Sometimes we'd get up from those lawn chairs and do a bunch of driving all around the county, all the time on red dirt. Not soil, mind you, or fields, but *dirt*. Oklahoma is dirty and red, and most of the cars you see in Oklahoma are all dirty and red. I love Oklahoma, don't get me wrong, I dearly love Oklahoma. It's just that when you've been away for a few years, you begin to realize how dirty and red the place really is. That's especially true when your research dumps you into that red dirt. But back to Glenn.

He knew all there was to know about cars, and he talked about them all the time, so about all you had to do was hang around and listen, and the next thing you knew you had all this information. Insight, too. I realize now that he had a way of teaching insight into machinery. Of course, when someone dies, a lot of people all wonder what it was he left that was of value. Oh, there's some property back in Oklahoma, but believe me when I say that of all the things he might have left, the most valuable was his gift to *me*. That gift consists of some insight into the workings of machinery. He taught me all I know about machines, especially Ford Automobiles, which I've found to be among the most educational of devices. He opened my eyes to the machinery that surrounds me in this most technological of ages: my television set, computers, center pivot sprinklers, electronic games that rumble away in the corner of my local bar, Peterbilt semis over on the highway—he could tell about them all in ways that made me begin to think of *living* things as machinery. In the end, he taught me all I know about machines, including some *living* ones. But don't make the mistake of thinking he taught me all *he* knew. No, that could never have happened. Most of what he knew is now down under the red dirt and wiry Bermuda grass of an Oklahoma cemetery.

Like I said, walking is rote exercise. There are many things about my profession that require rote exercise: glassware washing, making culture medium, recording grades, lots of things. I must be built like some machine with a bypass switch, for I find that rote exercise is one of the most productive of my activities. Rote exercise occupies the hands but frees the mind. Or in the case of a walk to Grand Island, it occupies the feet but frees the mind. A free mind can be a dangerous instrument. It wanders into places it's been kept out of for years, it returns to its birthplace, and it migrates to far countries with little respect for propriety. It does things it would not do were it occupied. Mine routinely synthesizes out of control, spewing into my internal milieu new combinations and permutations of recent experiences like some electronic racketball with a major short circuit. With Glenn in my thoughts, cars whipping by, tantalizingly, off on Interstate 80 a mile away, and my feet occupied by rote exercise, my mind began spewing out lists of human inventions, technical things, starting with the automobiles that had been the life focus of my friend.

It continued spewing with a list of human inventions, then a list of misuses of human inventions, and then extended that list to include things no one thought of as *inventions,* so misused were they out of ignorance and innocence. And as I walked, with Glenn's insight into machinery ringing in my memory, my runaway mind added to those lists additional lists of technical things that evil persons misused on purpose, that altruistic persons misused out of zeal, that zealous persons misused out of altruism or evility, righteous persons misused out of misunderstanding, lay people misused because of lack of technical education, children misused because they were not adults and adults misused because they were not children, primitives misused because they were primitive, specialists misused because of lack of breadth, and before long it just got tired of making these long lists of scientific and technical things misused by humans. It kicked back, went into reverse even as my feet stayed in forward, pushing me unerringly toward Grand Isle, and my first small flock of yellowlegs. In reverse, it began spewing out a list of technicons and humans that worked properly, in every way, every time, together. When the printout came, it was scribbled in beer-blurred writing on the back of a gas credit card receipt, and it contained only two items: "Glenn, the Master Mechanic" and "Ford Automobile."

There will be later parts of this tale in which we see how machine-age thinking has allowed the indiscriminate and uncontrolled application of technology to living things such as my Platte River. Soon I will begin to reveal my findings on the subject of watershed modeling, and you will discover from those findings that often machine-age thinking can operate as a feed-forward system, generating accelerating waves of machine-age thinking. In the end, I will tell you that this kind of thinking needs to be stopped immediately, and you will be surprised that a scientist holding a yellowlegs in his hand could decry our dependency upon technology. You will be even more surprised when that scientist tells you that of all species which must have a refuge if our human ecological niche is to remain intact, it is that species of thought which produces poets: The Romantic.

I learned all the above from a man who on the surface was one of the most classic of humans. Inside, however, he was one of the most romantic. He led the most classic of lives—understanding, fixing, manipulating machinery that few others could. He led it most successfully by being a romantic, never letting objective reductionist machine-age analytical thinking interfere with his *sense,* his *feel,* for what might be wrong with a Ford Automobile, our most familiar technicon. He turned me into a romantic, never letting objective reductionist machine-age analytical thinking override my *sense,* my *feel,* of what might be wrong with a human ecological niche that did not contain a lesser yellowlegs.

He only carried simple tools, a pair of pliers and a screwdriver in his pocket, and for that reason I walked that day a year ago with the simplest tools of *my* trade: binoculars, a white porcelain pan, a quarter-inch seine. He could fix almost anything on a Ford

Automobile with a pair of pliers and a screwdriver; and, I have come to know that I can study, and teach (= fix?) almost anything of significance in my world of living things with my simplest tools. He taught me *never* to assume that parts, if put together in correct order, sequence and structural relationship would indeed make car go. He taught me *always* to assume that parts would indeed make car go if put together with the proper amount of soul, an exact amount of oily disrespect, and the élan which invariably accompanies attack of a complicated machine with the simple tools. His name was "Glenn." In the end, they called him "Master Mechanic."

For example, Glenn said to me one time:

"Garage'll always make a profit, *always,* don't matter much what they sell out on the floor, garage'll *always* pay their bills, pay for the whole place. Unless, o' course, gets sloppy out there. Why I tell you I've got more business for that bunch up there than they'll ever know. Some guy comes in off the highway, has some little problem, I fix it with a screwdriver, don't send 'em no bill, next time that guy comes in and buys a new car. I seen it happen hundreds of times; thousands even."

"I do believe you, Glenn, I do believe you about the hundreds of times."

"People don't know how to take care of a car, never did, always mess it up somehow if they can. Well, that's okay, keeps me workin' up here. Oh, once in a while you'll get a bad one, not very often, but once in a while. I do remember one ole boy . . ." and his voice would trail off into a tale of some "ole boy" who actually got a bad Ford, what he did about it, how he, Glenn, tried to tell him it was just a bad car and that he should give it back to management, and on and on. And then would come tales of every major and minor thing, usually ending with the statement that he finally had to "overhaul her rear end." But through it all ran the thread of fact that not one of Glenn's cars ever gave him any trouble. Most were bought secondhand, including the Model T and Model A, reconditioned and stored away in a garage he'd built to house them. You might say Glenn was a secondhander. He also worked for a secondhander, one who used his insights but was uncomfortable in the presence of those insights, so who solved the problem with a $25 Christmas bonus and a gallon of cheap vodka out in the "shop" at New Year's.

After thirty years of this, Glenn had had enough. He "retired" early, making the equivalent of his bonus every day with minor tuneups, interest on loans. He fished the local farm ponds and like some living machine made them perform for him and him only with simple gear, got sick, went to the hospital, looked around at the medical machinery, tried to tell a nurse a peristaltic pump was not working properly, got an enema in return for the favor, and died. When he left, he left no name on the country club roster of his small town, he left no names on cards given to solicit business, he left no vacant seat on any church governing board, on any town council. He left instead my whole view of the age of technology and machinery. He left instead a vision which now burns in my mind in a way that cannot be extinguished, of the world as a complicated machine driven by a species that doesn't know how to take care of it.

I remember standing for a last long time on the banks of a red-mud farm pond down in Oklahoma where Glenn and I had fished the lunker bass, seeing the places along the shore which might still bear the impression of Glenn's body where he went to sleep that day, that lazy day, and deciding that if I were in the market for a planet, the vital signs of a good used machine would not be present and that I would close the hood of Earth, having seen beneath that hood the attitudes of previous owners, and not liking what I had seen. The truly frightening thing about all this is that there is no Ford garage, Glenn standing on greasy concrete, to which a planet could be taken.

Finally, on the day of his funeral, I could stand it no longer. I got behind the wheel of my car, left the crowd, and drove to the nearest farm pond where the early fall migrants were gathering. Bouncing across the pasture, hitting high center, prairie grass caught in the doors, I came upon the red earthen dam, the red banks, and the red water. My eyes searched the shore, searched for that link between man and Earth that had always functioned so well to return my thoughts to the wild planet, the Mother Earth in fine tune. My mind searched through all images in which to explain the effects this Master Mechanic was to have on my life until I found that burning vision of This Earth Planet as the Ultimate Machine driven by Classics, Classics who would drive it, reduce it, analyze it, manipulate it, and in the end junk it, unless shown the Romantic in some as yet unenvisioned way. And I sorted through the species that gather at Oklahoma farm ponds these times of year until I found the one that had always, as a child, taken me to new places of the imagination. There, working its way along the shore, was a lesser yellowlegs.

That all took place a year ago. Those experiences may have been a factor contributing to my decision to take leave, for those experiences and visions have occupied my mind incessantly for the last year. Those thoughts and visions had to lead to that decision to become an ecologist. High and mighty thoughts I had a year ago, didn't I? How many of you, I wonder, on your way to Colorado, back to Chicago, looked over at me in the fields near Grand Island, with my professor wardrobe—pan, seine, the simple tools of my trade—slung over a shoulder, and had any inkling of the high and mighty thoughts that were spinning through my brain?

It took three, four, five days—I don't remember exactly—a year ago to reach Grand Island. There were a great many barbed-wire fences to climb, it seemed, and some little creeks to explore and some rain puddles to search between here and Grand Island. The Platte River and Interstate 80 meet near that city. You can see from a great distance that you are approaching Grand Island in the spring and fall. The skyline of Grand Island is rather plain, hidden off north of I-80, and you can't really see the skyline. You know, however, without any doubt that you are approaching the place where the river meets the road. Great clouds of waterfowl tell you that. They circle over that line of cottonwoods and can be seen for many miles. Where there are waterfowl along a river, there must also be the yellowlegs. My lessons for the machine age, those burning visions from a Master Mechanic in hand, my walking was no longer rote exercise! The river was in sight!

4 ⌐ First Flock

*. . . the birds will often fly back and forth
over him or even alight on the ground near him.*

A. C. Bent

I arrived upon the Platte at night; those turning clouds of
waterfowl came closer too slowly as I plodded. I shunned the
highway, but off to my right in the deepening twilight I could see
Erma's Desire, a monumental piece of abstract sculpture marking
Grand Island, the place where the river meets the road. *Erma's
Desire* is artist John Raimondi's gift to the prairie people, with
angles and spires of Cor-ten steel, the sharpest and heaviest one
pointing west, my chosen direction, too. From the night above
came the hard pumping of duck wings, big duck wings, such as
mallards would have, and from the night ahead came the sound of
water moving. The Platte! I had come to become an ecologist, and I
was on the Platte where one can be nothing but an ecologist!

The decision to study yellowlegs had not been made then; that
decision was to come later. Thinking back now, trying to explain
the forces that actually made me choose to study this one animal, I
can see that first night near Grand Island was also the time of no
return. It might have been easy to return the eighty-eight miles the
next morning, had I started before daybreak. But by the time light
revealed those shifting sands the next morning, my ability to catch
a bus homeward had been destroyed. There were nightmares; I'll
tell you about those. But the morning brought relief. It came in

34

over the cottonwoods. There were three of them that brought that relief, and they worked their ways along the edge of an isolated pool a hundred yards from where I lay.

Intelligent people say some pretty stupid things sometimes, so it doesn't bother me to say this: my nightmares were caused by the whistle of wind through a large pipe containing a flow gauge. Those dreams all related to that gauge, to extensions of its meaning, so they must have been caused by the wind. I've had some of those dreams since, too, and they are ones I never had before that night eighty-eight miles from home, so I know their origin was in the wind. Of all the other sounds that were on the wind that night, none of them generated any nightmares. I dream of no giant mallards chasing me, no willowy call strikes terror in my sleeping heart, no insistent whisper of the Platte grows into the scream of ghosts, no yelp of coyote sets me shivering. No, those things make me smile, especially today. But the wind in the gauge pipe, it had special meaning coming so close upon my memories of the Master Mechanic and his essence.

The Platte drains an area of almost ninety thousand square miles. Three hundred more miles to the west it's but a trickle. Out where it crosses the state line, it averages about seven or eight hundred cubic feet of water a second. That seems like a lot, but it's just a trickle. A cubic foot of water weighs sixty-two pounds. That means that out there at the state line where this river is just a trickle, it's still delivering twenty-two tons of water a second. The land falls from the headwaters at the rate of about six feet a mile. By the time the river reaches the other state line, the one at the eastern end, it's delivering about six thousand cubic feet a second. That's a hundred eighty-six tons of water every second. There are times, say in June after spring rains, when it delivers almost forty thousand cubic feet of water a second. That's a thousand two hundred forty tons of water. Every second.

When you wade in the Platte, you are touching a moving thing, you are touching a machine that is moving untold amounts of heavy materials every second, that is several hundred miles long, a mammoth snake across the prairie, an energy-force big and strong and all powerful. I've felt at times the river doesn't like to be touched; it moves sand away from beneath my feet. It tries very gently to move itself, to get away, but it's so large and powerful and intent upon its own business, and I'm so small, that before long the river ends up doing exactly the opposite of what it tried. It tries to politely excuse itself, but before long the sand has washed up around my ankles and instead of excusing itself, the river has trapped me, is holding me. I've found in the last year that the river has other ways of trapping humans; it catches their minds and hearts. That's what it was like wading in the river upon which I began my education as an ecologist.

The river is wide, and it has a channel that may be small, but that channel wanders over a bed that is wide. The river is long, and its tributaries are long. Its length and width are two dimensions. Thickness is a third dimension. If you cut this mighty river across in thousands of places along its main channel, its tributaries, its headwaters, and looked at the places you cut, you'd see a wall of water, flat on top, bent to the angle of the bed below. You'd see the shape of the bed, the kinds of soils that make up that bed and the land beneath it, the river's connections to the water-bearing sand beneath it. And every place the river was cut, the area of that cross-section could be calculated, the area of the various kinds of soils, the cross-sectional area of water, and from those figures you could calculate flow rates and volumes, the amount of water that could be stored in soils beneath the sand, and on and on. And you would then have measured the third dimension of the Platte.

The fourth dimension of the Platte is time, and there have been times when I thought that dimension was infinite. No longer do I think that. At some time in geological history, the Platte was born. At some time in my lifetime, I would not be surprised to see the Platte die. These comments are not controversial nor new. They were expressed on national television for all to see when one of the networks presented James Michener's *Centennial*. They are written between the lines of every Environmental Impact Statement filed from this part of the country, if not from all the West.

The flow-gauge pipe, channeling the dark wind for those long hours that first night, represented to me all this measurement of the Platte. That pipe measured in some way the dimensions of that river, measured its flow every hour, every day, continuously. I don't know how often those measurements are taken. I had visions of an army of such pipes, marching down upon the Platte, measuring the pulse of my river—yes, the pulse, the very pulse—maybe, I thought, to find the vein, the artery, in order to punch in a needle to drain the land's lifeblood. Those numbers must all be recorded somewhere, probably in some computer file, and read out when needed. I envision that printout easily: it makes a very thick book with chapters telling the numbers of the seasons, the numbers of life's events. This list of numbers, especially the list of weekly averages, would tell you of the spring thaw, when those twelve hundred tons of water a second are filthy, almost black, with accumulated oil and grease and exhaust dust of a billion car-miles, lifted from the city streets with urban pack ice, uncovering axle-busting holes as it melts, sending that river melt water down city sewers into some hapless tributary, then into this river. Yes, indeed—the March weekly average cubic-feet-per-second flow is written in snow-melt black type!

You could see the rains, some blockbuster rains, in the April numbers, and if you had the daily averages, you could see not only the rains but how rapidly the water ran off into this river, which farmer's land held the most water. The tributary flows would tell you that and where the soils were most porous and thus held back the rainwater. Yes, indeed—an April shower would be right there in the printout illustrated as some cfs figure for some week in April. In June, the numbers would peak, and you could read violent storms in those numbers, violent storms that bring out the spadefoot toads. They only breed when the storms are especially violent, storms so violent they frighten a human—that's what brings a spadefoot out of the ground to find a mate! Cutest toads anyone ever saw! What a thunderous psyche there must be beneath that wrinkled skin, what a primeval sex-drive there must be inside that little balloon that it should be aroused only when the sirens tell humans to take shelter from extremes! You could open that printout book, turn to the cfs average for the first week of June and see the spadefoots breeding, if you knew how to look. It's all in the numbers.

The numbers are stored in a computer data file. As everyone knows, the computer is our finest machine, which is probably why I was able to make the connections between the gauge pipe and the

Master Mechanic's message about machinery. Or, I should say, my subconscious was able to make that connection. I don't have nightmares on purpose. But I should describe the circular movements of my nightmares that night. Those circular movements concerned rivers, numbers, computers, and values, and although they may have started with the night wind, they quickly became a cartwheel galaxy through my mind, in which engineers measured my river, recorded those measurements in a computer, then wrote a program to explain those fluctuating numbers, then in a fit of playfulness, they began doing what kids do best with models: playing, toying, manipulating, and teaching other kids to do the same things, so that computer manipulation of the model watershed became a game in itself.

My nightmares never ended so easily as some games with lesser toys. Man's finest machine turned toy, it functioned in my dreams exactly as any toy functions—it set the values of those who played with it. Give a little girl a doll, tell her all little girls play with dolls all their life, and you've set their values forever. Give a little boy a gun, tell him either directly or indirectly that all little boys play guns, and he grows up thinking it's a natural thing to play guns. Give a little boy a computer with a river inside, tell him it's important to be able to manipulate that toy river, tell him that storms are the greatest events, and you've generated a kid who sees little wrong with manipulating a river. A *real* river. You've set his values forever. Never mind that he was in his twenties when you gave him his model.

My dreams never finish easily. Tell that kid what he is doing is high technology, make him a professional at his games, and the next thing you know he's generating more just like himself. A positive feed-forward system. Its products in turn generate more products, and the next thing you know those products are generating products, and you have an accelerating wave of kids who see only the numbers in their finest machines, who see their role as a manipulator of ecosystems, for if there is anything their finest toy has allowed them to do, it's manipulate concepts, like a braided prairie river, that were too large for our minds only a few years ago. So I know that although I can pick up that printout and see the spadefoots breeding, they can't. The Classic has come to be blind to the Romantic. That would never have happened to a Master Mechanic, even with the finest of machines.

I was covered with sand, I know from those nightmares of runaway Classic that I must have writhed through the night out there on the sand bar. But morning from the middle of a braided river was wondrous to behold. Thousands of birds I was never able to identify flittered through the tops of tall cottonwoods, jumping among twigs, making patterns across a band of sky to more tall cottonwoods on the other side. Kingfisher rattled across downstream then back across, a scratch drawn on the new day. Great blue heron came with wings set, giant sky shadow of blue-gray, turning in glide down between the cottonwoods, along that sky ribbon above my head, wings set, air whistling through a bale of flight feathers, legs dangling this way and that, long plumes blowing in the glide wind, head with evil eyes searching shallow running stream for a frog place. But where for me to begin upon the Platte? Where to begin my studies of ecology, which relationship, with which species? Where does one start taking when one is surrounded by an infinite sea of what one wants?

Full of such questions, still fitful from the Classic nightmares, I sought relief everywhere—in the heron, in the schools of small fishes, in the waves of mayflies, but as I reported at the beginning of this chapter, relief came in low over the cottonwoods instead, turning and cutting with pointed wings as they always do, calling soft but insistent the willowy call that had come from the night hours earlier, *pill-e-wee, pill-e-wee,* turning sharply downward onto the edge of one of those isolated pools for which the Platte is famous. Yellowshanks! For me at the time, almost a year ago, the United States Cavalry could not have been more welcome!

They stayed for an hour, and there were three of them, my childhood dreams out there on the Platte, over along that isolated pool. I could make no other decision than to follow these birds, or at least some, or even one, like them. When they left, they flew west into the late morning, and I had no choice but to follow. They took the road of the pioneers, along the Platte west, but when they left, they left at thirty or forty miles an hour. I still walked the road of the pioneers, but always in their direction, west, past Grand Island where the river meets the road, west of Grand Island where the river *is* the road, west with something to follow, something I felt was of value to my budding career as an ecologist, a first flock of three lesser yellowlegs. I didn't have enough sense to look for a band at the time. I'm a better ecologist than that now; I look for a band every day.

5 ᔓ Banded Lady

This ring! . . . How, how on earth did it come to me?
Ah! . . . That is a very long story.

Frodo Baggins and
the Wizard Gandalf

I'm sure there are those of you who have never seen a bird band, much less placed one on some migratory thing. These bands are silver-bright aluminum when they're new, but when they're old, they have a mystique that cannot be described; it must be felt. I have often wondered who manufactures bird bands, who runs the computer programs that decide which numbers go on which series, and on and on goes my wondering about bird bands. But that wondering is only a fraction of the wondering that accompanies discovery of a band on a wild bird. These bands are smooth, the aluminum is sometimes dark and worn, often dirt fills the numbers. This last is especially true if the species is one that frequents the mud. You immediately wonder how long that band, that old band, has been there, and where in the world that band has been. But most of all, you wonder who it was that put that thing on.

Banded sandpipers are very rare. We won't discuss this feeling I have that sandpipers produce some kind of emotional backlash in a bander, some kind of feeling that the bird should not be banded, else a symbol of wilderness will be diminished. Nevertheless, banded waders are rare. Don't get your hands on a sandpiper very

41

often to band it, that's probably the reason. They tend not to fly into nets in wholesale numbers like some warblers, finches, blackbirds, orioles. No; instead, they tend to stay far out on the flats, coming and leaving along unpredictable paths through the prairie air. Most sandpiper banding probably happens up on the nesting grounds, up north, where only a special breed of people get their hands on a baby yellowlegs, maybe press that aluminum anklet in place and send that chick back out into the weeds.

I suppose my thoughts were on sandpiper chicks and nests that morning west of Grand Island. I have often wondered where those birds came from; no, I don't mean a recent flight, say from South Dakota, but the deeper source, the nesting grounds, the genetic stock, the time in geological history, that portion of the planet known to zoogeographers as the "center of origin." There must be some source of sandpipers. I know now that there *must* be a source of sandpipers and maybe even of people to band them, but again I don't mean *just* a source, but a deeper source, a place in that human consciousness, perhaps, that functions as a source by demanding of itself that there always *be* sandpipers to walk the prairie mudflats.

Of course, I've also wondered where they go, but that morning west of Grand Island there was little question in my mind where they'd gone; west, they'd gone west along the Platte. How uneducated could a university professor have been, as I was a year ago, assuming they'd only gone west! What an age of innocence that week was, walking the sands of the Platte west, wondering at the source of yellowlegs, convinced I knew they were heading west and thinking little beyond that! In retrospect now, that innocence worked to my advantage, for I kept following that river west into the deeper prairies, little knowing that those deeper prairies were to be the source of *my* sandpiper, the *one* which has pointed me in the direction I must follow these years. Now that we've mentioned the one, this is probably also a good time to pull together some of the results of my research over the last year and dip into biology. I wondered then about the source of yellowlegs, and as we walk the Platte deeper into the plains, let me tell you the results of my wondering, the summary of my investigations into the source of sandpipers, the nesting location from which a single banded gray lady was to fly into my life with the force of an intergalactic expedition.

This home of a banded sandpiper, this nesting location, was in Canada, near the end of the woods and stuck down in weeds not far from a fallen snag. It was a shallow depression, with a few carefully placed leaves arranged as only a mother yellowlegs can arrange them for babies that could care less for a thing called a "nest." The area was wooded only in places, with many scrags of small dead trees lifting broken arms across the landscape to a leaden sky. The water was near, for water is always near for a sandpiper, and there were four eggs, flecked with bile, dried, turned, sat upon. The explosion of life within those eggs could only be understood by one who had watched it. The rush to live was rarely equaled when a sandpiper chick decided to enter the northern wilderness as a weightless fluff. Everything is rushed in the northland. A certain disrespect for time pervades the life of breeding creatures, and for one with an experience of long months of southern springs, the impatience of a northern breeder can not be told; it must be witnessed.

Her chick was nothing against the wild. Held in the human hand within two minutes of hatching, it could be crushed into a bloody down pulp by accidental good intentions. But life was there in the wilderness to be grasped, lived for however long or short time is allotted, and the chick was ready. More than the human hand that holds it would ever be. The fluff had a special structure on its bill to aid it in ripping through the eggshell. What fraction of all given strength resources must have been expended to even see the light of day! What fury must have been raised in that infinitesimal heart by parent peeps and calls heard through an eggshell, calling the chick inside into a world of sunlight and hungry ermine! The structure was known as an egg tooth and it covered the tips of both the upper and lower bills. It would be used once for the sole purpose of getting through a shell, then discarded. The egg tooth was the technological equivalent of a monstrous controlled fire-bomb skyscraper Saturn rocket—used once to get into the world of flight then discarded! The one of the lower bill, however, was only for protection. As equipment for the northern wilderness nature had given a yellowlegs chick a bill so weak and flexible that it had to give it another bill on top of that one just to get through the shell and still another to protect the lower mandible while the upper mandible was chipping and cutting through what must have seemed like a sheet of hardened steel.

The scientific literature does not state whether her chick rested after making the first breakthrough to daylight. There is probably a reason for this hiatus: no chick was *ever* ready to rest after the initial pip through—to rest might mean not to survive. The sight of daylight could only drive this thing to further frenzy, systematic frenzy. The shell fell apart and there it sat, precocial thing of the wild, ready for a world in which a flight to Argentina in three months was expected. Until airborne, the chick was not to communicate very much in sound but was to respond to a spectrum of parental calls. Little fluff had practiced this last; it had been freezing motionless within the egg at the sound of parental alarm for at least a day or two. Habit well-formed indeed! The morning's light might have revealed a scavenging gull, and the parental call would turn the chick into a soundless speckled rock.

Within two minutes, its eyes were opened and it blinked at the horizon, turning its head first to the south. Ten minutes later its head was up and body tempered. Half an hour later it was on its feet and by the end of the first hour of life had pecked at something in the nest. Before the day was over, it would walk and soon thereafter would run. What a task for a parent to take care of such disrespect for helplessness! The one tool was a whistle, and with it a circling mother could freeze her brood until another was given, an all-clear. This freezing would happen many times a day for the next week or so and would be about the only positive control a parent could exert over running determination, legs growing stronger by the minute, eyes picking up hapless larvae with increasing ferocity, still fuzzy wings thrust in defiance at the wind, primary feathers adding to the defiance by the hour. Such freezing was carefully compartmentalized, however, for there were times when a whistle was not enough, and the chick ran to a parent's wing, put itself completely under the protection of the parent, itself frail stuff against cruising fox.

By the end of the first day, she had three of those downy chicks, all achieving "full teeter" within thirty minutes of hatching. The fourth egg did not hatch. We have no way of knowing whether there was a struggling chick inside, losing its first battle for survival, fully formed, ready, responding to a parental call, only the thickness of an egg shell away from a full life. The egg may simply have been infertile. If given the choice of explanation as to why her fourth egg had not hatched, the banded lady would have chosen infertility. Troubles enough she would expect on the next day, without having the added guilt of knowing a fully developed living chick was an eggshell away from life, especially when one considered the energy investment she had in that egg. So at the end of the first day, she rested. Tomorrow she would have three real twits on her hands and by the end of the second day would be exhausted.

Of course, there was that strange experience waiting for her first thing on the second day. A man would pursue one of her chicks through the grass and catch it, taking it into a tent. This sort of thing had happened in years past, old man, fox, jaeger, it didn't matter—she never had finished the month of July with all her chicks. But even a stranger thing happened later on the second day. He returned her chick, stooping with a grin to let the little thing run out of his cupped hand into the grass, where immediately it froze to the whistle of a parent circling. The man returned to his tent, where he picked up a board with a single sheet of heavy paper taped to it and took the board out into the light. He had a paintbrush in one hand, a watercolor brush, and there on the paper was her firstborn chick, fluffy, downy, defiant, looking back over its shoulder, outlandish legs, full teeter indeed, recorded for all human posterity and for all humans who would never hold the sandpiper chick. The man looked at the painting and smiled. These newly hatched chicks were always unruly, and this one had been no exception. Total exasperation it was, trying to concentrate on the painting while keeping track of the model. He had come to understand the plight of a parent yellowlegs many years before, and he had no wish to be responsible for a sandpiper chick for two or three weeks!

The act of choosing a baby sandpiper to paint was an act that sent crackles of value electricity throughout one's life. A human who painted a bird's picture was a human who had given up something to become a part of earth-machine now turning, groaning with the weight of tankers, screaming from the cuts and slashes of mines, choking with the smoke of plastic trinkets, crying in anguish over the rhinoceros carcass now rotting, ripped by hyenas after its heart was blasted to tissue fragments by a high-powered rifle with only an aphrodisiac horn in mind. The man returned to the tent and brought out a small stool, replaced his paper, dipped his brush, licked the tip into a point a few times, and quickly sketched the sunset of the second day. In the fading light, he added some of the far, low hills and their shadow patterns. Through his binoculars, he had seen that the mother yellowlegs was banded, and that observation affected him in a way no other had or would for years to come. He was unique among humans. He had come to the north, set up his tent, captured a yellowlegs chick, painted the most uncooperative little creature in a defiant pose—had looked almost disbelieving, his breath taken away—at the parent standing yammering on the tree stump. There had been a silver band on her ankle; he had seen it for sure then worked himself closer to confirm it. At the end of the second day, he noted in pencil on the bottom of the chick's picture that its parent had a band, but the bird had not been "collected," so that the band's number was of course unknown. The man lay in his sleeping bag that night late, and the drawing board with its sketch of wilderness leaned against the tent pole. There were five billion people on earth-machine at the time. Each and every one of them needed to be with him that night.

The time of summer passed with a rush in Canada, but with each day the three survivors ranged faster and further afoot, scooting through tall grass, past an occasional withered small tree, and along the edge of the bog. The man and his tent had gone from their small wilderness, and he had bothered them no more after the second day. There were things these chicks did because of some inner messages from their brains, messages over which they had no control. These inner messages told them which larvae to pick up, the type of plants their down would blend most closely with, how to place their feet, their posture, their competitive relationships, how to look for the sun and where to go at night. There were also things they learned: directions to the water's edge, which shadows to be afraid of, the textures of their environments to be avoided, and the songs and whistles of some other birds. The vocal repertoire of their mother also became cultural enrichment, for they were beginning now at quiet and safe times to imitate her calls, and one of them added some notes that were not really intended to be yellowlegs notes. This last, of course, was a slight sign of rebellion, unhindered thinking—this vocal act of stepping out of the bounds allowed yellowlegs. Another form of cultural enrichment, unhindered thinking, rebellion, exhibited by this particular chick was not allowed a yellowlegs, although who was to say that it didn't have to happen. Maybe this was the way little yellowlegs learned the real lessons of life, such as how far to stay away from the average shrub. This bundle of adolescent beauty, one of the single most endearing animals to be found on earth, was pinned to the ground in a blinding flash of fox paws, and its last view of the world was the slavering inside of a mouth as it crushed her head and body into a bloody mass of down and pinfeathers. The speed was merciful. The fox crushed once, killing the little bird, then bit quickly three or four times, snapping its head forward in the manner of all dogs each time, and all that remained of the running rebellious chick, all that remained of expended parent energy and of the model whose picture now graced watercolor paper was some blood around the mouth of a Canadian fox. The fox licked a few times, staring into the grass where its bird had been. The death of their sister was witnessed by the other two and the parent. Yellowlegs are not totally dumb. The remaining chicks stayed closer to the water, where they expressed their disrespectful ideas in other ways.

The first flights were interesting. It is not recorded whether the banded lady had a moment of parental anxiety, such as might attend a human parent's first permission for teenager to solo the family car. The first flights were small things, really extensions of runs along the shore, testings of unslotted primaries and sharpened eyes. The wings themselves had been tested almost since hatching; it was only after the first few feathers grew that these same movements began to take on significance. The first lift-off came as a total surprise to first one then the other of the surviving chicks. Watching the brood, the man would have concluded that these young things knew exactly what a wing was for, but he had gone by the time of the first lift-off. He knew exactly what to look for on the face of a bird, too, so he would have seen the total surprise the first time feet actually left the ground. He would also have seen both chicks fall while landing the first time. The first flight was about two feet in length. The second was also about two feet. The third was about ten feet and by the time the adolescents had left the ground twenty times they were no longer fox food. By the end of the day, they were flying, out over the water, in circles, across the bog, out to the marsh, where they roosted that night with the parent, hardly able to sleep with their newfound freedom, planning nothing but flying, maybe faraway, maybe faraway from the parent forever with the hyperboreal morning.

First after it in the morning was a male, and he preened and poked in the water and tried a couple of short hops before the sun actually warmed the air. They still worked, these wings designed for a flight to Argentina, even now beginning to take shape in this chick's subconscious, and he activated the FLIGHT program and was off, following the water's edge, every stroke gaining in strength and confidence when he, the second of my yellowlegs' chicks, exploded. He never saw the falcon. It struck from above with knotted fists from a dive that might have started a mile high, and this chick on his first *real* flight simply exploded in a cloud of small feathers, gray and white feathers, was grabbed by those same spiked feet before he'd fallen a yard, and was carried beyond the horizon to an aerie to feed the ornery brood of an endangered species. The falcon was almost a mile away before the last of the gray feathers touched the water, where they floated, drifting apart, pushed toward the shore by the slightest of breeze.

The last of the remaining chicks also flew, this time moving far away from the banded lady parent. He alone would reach the *pampas* and he alone of the four eggs would return to this the death spot for brother and sister. His mother, who had also started her life so many years ago in this very place, would not return next year. She was destined to end up in my hands at the close of my year, pointing her long bill into my future, me then unable to resist the directions of the yellowlegs, the call of the yellowlegs, the commands of yellowlegs. But from the Keewatin that summer a year ago, she came anyway. Any prior knowledge of her fate would never have stopped her, for yellowlegs do what they must do regardless. She left that nest location, one day there, one day gone, and flew into my life at forty miles an hour, piercing thermals, racing across national boundaries, through the night, through the early morning, toward a mudflat and a meeting with a scientist. How simple it all sounds now!

6 ⁀ On the Flats

*Although always alert and easily alarmed,
it is not noticeably shy.*

Thomas Burleigh

Sunrise over the dunes was a beautiful thing. There was a special light over the land in those moments when sunlight diffused through spider webs and heavy dew. She had flown through the special light earlier, but the sun had risen to flash off her wings, and the dew had steamed from the dry beneath her. The earless lizards now warmed their trusting bodies against the side of a blowout, and a burrowing owl sat on a telephone pole connecting the Glinn Ranch with a wire leading to the ends of the plains. Gray bird with trailing yellow legs came out of the night skies through the special light into the August of Sandhills. Yucca and bluestem passed beneath her; she did not notice. Once a mile there was a well, often with a crowd of burgundy cattle, pawing sand around a dripping tank. Once every few miles there was a marsh, a wet place in the sand, cattails, sedges, maybe some open water, and she might have stopped at one of these places were it not for the miles of mudflat she could see in her mind over the horizon. It would be very hot later that August day out on the plains, and she would feel the heat rising from the dunes as she caught sight of miles of open water a dozen miles away.

She rarely stopped here in the spring. Somehow the urgency to return home overrode many feelings, and the pothole stops were the barest necessities in the spring. This was fall, however, a season of responsibilities lifted, a season of lingering. Besides, for three months, humans had been dumping water out of this reservoir as rapidly as the law would allow. Miles of open ground, open mud, often miles from the nearest brush where fox or mink or little boy with rifle hid, awaited her in the fall. The lingering place was this flat, a place to spend the days and cooling evenings with friends, with solitary sandpipers, relatives, erratic pectorals, perhaps placed on earth for the entertainment of other sandpipers, with willets and avocets, the big boys, turning wings, gliding, and with ducks and geese she knew to be different from herself. A fear always came into her heart with ducks and geese, perhaps the fear of a human watching men marching off to war with real guns, for she had seen the ducks and geese fold in the air and fall, she had seen their bloody wings and heads out on the mudflats, and she knew they were a different creature from herself. She flew when ducks and geese came; they put a fear into her that she could not control so went away, down the shore many hundreds of yards to a place where the fear subsided and fish fry swam in clouds beneath a murky surface.

It was mid-morning and ninety degrees when she came to the mudflats. The air was total stillness, and the sounds of motorboat and quacking feeding duck came from many miles down the lake. Out on the water, two fishermen sat and talked. She set her wings into a long glide, pumped a few times, and came to rest in a place where her feet made little prints. The water was receding slowly; the prints would be dry by afternoon and fixed in the mud. Under other conditions they might have become perfect fossils, mixed in with the thousands of footprints of dozens of other species that shared the mud with her. What a symphony score of sandpiper and plover footprints, trills, crescendos, full chords, rests, runs Liszt himself would have been proud of, repeats, some soft and some *forte!* What a puzzle for some future paleontologist! What a puzzle to sort out the meanings of all those dashes, starts, stops and steps! She left her footprints in soft mud, and she stepped across hard places, she waded directly into water alive with a taxonomist's life work and ate undescribed species of insects by the gram. She swallowed little fishes whole, and she drank some of the half mud.

51

She was weary as only a migrating bird can be weary in the minds of humans who seriously consider such a feat. She slept that afternoon, fed again, slept that night, and spent lazy days of a perfect Indian Summer on the mudflats at the upper end of a large large reservoir.

It was the fertile time of all years, this Indian Summer, with the minute progeny of plains creatures taking their chances for a development and winter survival challenge still several months away. Food for a sandpiper, that's all they were, the microcrustacea swarming in that murk, only food for sandpipers, or maybe for little fishes that were themselves only food for sandpipers. There grubbed in the mud a kind of insect no man had ever seen, although the mudflat was in the middle of the most civilized and most highly technical society ever evolved. She ate that undescribed species with not the slightest knowledge or feeling for a scientist sitting in a laboratory a hundred miles away. While she rested, her only surviving chick flew over her and on to another mudflat in another state, a prairie state. She would not have recognized him had he landed beside her. She was old, she had been to Argentina several times and was in no hurry to get there again, in no hurry to test the Gulf of Mexico again, in no hurry to run the gauntlet of Mexican hunters who would consume her dark breast in three bites if they could only get their hands on her. She would eat and rest as she had done before in the fall. The band on her leg caught on a small twig in the water, and she shook her foot to free it.

Her life was, and had been always, the extremes. She had done things humans had only longed to do, and she had done things that humans were fearful of. She had traveled and seen the countryside like no human would ever see it, the details of a mudflat, the details of a river, patterns from the low altitude no human in a sealed jumbo jet thirty thousand feet above could ever study. She experienced the changing patterns of earth slowly, too, and her distance flights were to the airliner what walking is to the automobile. Walking, compared to a Ford Automobile, is cold, slow, hot, muscle powered, but none of these things is the *real* difference between walking and riding. No, walking one saw things in a city one never saw from a car window. Ladies hanging laundry or sunbathing, dogs, the patterns of diseased grass in an ill-kept lawn, a broken red wagon alongside a broken front porch, the total richness of an environment sensed at slow speeds from a different value set—that is the difference between walking and riding. Thus yellowlegs had things no human could ever have. She inherited these things, and among them was a view of the earth simply not technologically available to a scientist on leave.

Yellowlegs had traveled. Her flights would have cost the life savings of a couple now into their seventies, having worked for the phone company. And she had received more for her budgeted energy expenditures than would the phone company couple. The damping effects of convenience technology were things she had never felt. One could experience the full range of Earth just by flying to Argentina, with one's own wings, that is. The minute texture of her environmental niche from Canada to South America was something she experienced twice a year, but it was not the same in the spring as in the fall. Oh, what man would be so fortunate! What fortune, to fly with the yellowlegs; fly over the Gulf with your own wings; fly along the shore of Padre Island; fly through skimmers and laughing gulls; fly to Yucatán; watch the Brazilian jungle, Solomon's mine of hummingbird jewels, slowly pass beneath you, and every bit as tangible as the front yards, dogs, dripping cars and broken ride toys of a midwestern America passing before a walking scientist on leave! It is not so simple as you think, dirt-bound human. A migration with sandpipers would alter a person, and the added year would be the least of changed ways!

There were other yellowlegs on the mudflats, although none other was banded, and she joined them loosely at times, wandered alone at other times, and a few other times flew in the most casual of formations off to the other end of the mud. There were solitary sandpipers, and once on a small spit of point there had been three together in the space of a few yards. The movements of her environment always registered in her sensory receptors, for the movements were signs, so the movements of three *solitaries* in defined space captured her attention. They were greatly annoyed with one another, rushing to and fro, even flailing at one another until the non-group disintegrated and two of the three flew away. In different directions. Only then did the remaining bird feed. She watched him for a few moments, then waded on. There were dowitchers, birds of incredible beauty, very long bills, and she liked dowitchers. She had no knowledge of the tapeworms inside every one of these dowitchers, a special kind of tapeworm that was as much a part of the word "dowitcher" as was bill length, and she had even less knowledge of other parasites, of other species, or of other obligations of other species, that were so inescapable as to become a part of those species's names. Dowitchers gave her a sense of security, a feeling of proper ecosystem functioning. The willets, big boys, held little place in her hierarchy of associates: all they ever seemed to do was sleep. The peeps were there for entertainment. The crazed pectorals never failed to catch her attention for long periods of time. She often watched for twenty or thirty minutes, and she often watched the leasts and Baird's to see if they did the same stupid things, but they never did. Had she been able to extend her observations into analysis and philosophy, she might have wondered how, in the world of sandpipers, a species could afford to make the decision to be a pectoral sandpiper.

I have often wondered similar thoughts: how can a man, in this time of unemployment, inflation, launched real estate costs and taxes, new homes beyond the reach of the average citizen of this land, college educations only dream of parents, pollution, traffic, responsibilities that consume the very matrix of a body—*how* can a man in these times actually make the decision to become an ecologist? I often extend my thoughts: there will always be insurance salesmen, mechanics, electricians, teachers. Will the human experiment also give rise inevitably to ecologists? To ornithologists? Scientists might well have asked questions similar in structure: given the sandpiper experiment, will there always be types such as pectorals, types such as yellowlegs, types such as the big boys sleeping out on the mud? I now know full well that if earth-machine is functioning properly then yes—the human experiment will inevitably give rise to ornithologists. Yellowlegs could never make the same conclusions about her relatives. She knew they were there, and by their behaviors as well as the planet signs she routinely monitored, she knew the upper mudflat of this great lake was the place for her to stay and wait. She waited for she knew not what, but the planet signs said "wait" and she obeyed.

We will never know, will we, whether she would have actually waited, or instead flown hurriedly on to South America, had the planet signs told the entire message. We will never know, will we, whether she would have stayed on that mudflat, leaving those footprints, had she known that some scientist was also out leaving footprints along the Platte, being led to her by members of her own kind, led to his meeting with his future. We will never know whether she would have instead flown hurriedly on to South America had the planet signs told the entire message: that she *was* this man's future.

7 ↔ To the Flats

An afternoon on the water might be a
bridge to their ultimate mission.

Norman Mailer

I have seen things in and on the Platte River that need to be reported, for they are things so few have ever seen. They have been revealed through use of the simple tools of my trade, applied to a vast force so mammoth it must be felt, for it cannot be understood, and these are the things I now teach when I teach the Platte, for I am now the ecologist I set out to be. These are the things I felt those long days beneath that unbanded flock of three, following that road of the pioneers, a road that led those pioneers into their futures, and a road that led me into my future a hundred and fifty years later.

Is there not a lesson here for us all? This river through the prairies, this river of life through these rolling dunes, has for so many generations been that avenue into the future, but throughout those generations that river has been wild. There is some feeling I have that when a river is tamed, it may no longer be that avenue into the future, any more than some wild spirit anywhere can serve as an avenue into the future from a position of servitude. We tame this wild spirit by stealing her water, like some parasite, sharing her very life's blood, using her, putting her to work in our fields of agriculture, controlling her floods, secure in our new relationship with a wild thing whose potential has been "tapped," whose wild spirit no longer washes away our belongings. It remains to be seen whether a wild thing now servile can also be an avenue into anyone's future. But I have seen that wilderness of the Platte from beneath her cottonwoods, and she has taken me west to the flats for that meeting with my future. But whether she can do that for each of you, I do not know. I see her wilderness with my simple tools. Who knows, maybe there is no wilderness left in her. Maybe I only see the wilderness because I am convinced it is there; maybe that wilderness is only in my mind. Maybe a wilderness of the mind can also be that avenue into the future.

Enough of this rambling. Here are my notes on the wilderness of the Platte; my brute expression of the wilderness that leads to banded yellowlegs and thence to the fine state of Kansas. Rather, that fine state of mind that accompanies the ultimate relationship with wilderness, the ultimate understanding of wilderness. Kansas might come close, but it's not the ultimate.

There was a small coffee shop in a small town, open through the night, shaking with the rolling thunder of boxcars, boxcars full of wheat at three in the morning, and then with the sound of semis shifting down for some stretch up, semis full of wheat, cattle, and cars for exchange. You can sit in those coffee shops at three in the morning and manipulate the river in your mind as easily as you can with a computer, but the river comes out in images, usually fleeting, sometimes lasting, or impressions, rather than in numbers or graphics, but still it's manipulation of the river. You can see the river never sleeping, only changing its ways slightly during the night, so that you think *it* is sleeping but really, even though it's resting from its day tasks, it's still awake. You can see it out there now changing its channel, moving some sand here and there, maybe drying a sand bar, maybe making a place for small fish to spawn and thousands of microscopic fry to survive, shallow warm to knee-deep and cold. You can see the insects sleeping, the swallows under the bridge sleeping or gone for the winter, raccoons picking picking along, leaving traces of a raccoon never seen.

It's quiet out there now, but in the earliest daylight when you walk out there, you still get the feeling that the river's been doing things during the night. There may be warblers high in the cottonwoods that weren't there the day before, and you don't know where they came from. There may be a soft-shelled turtle up in some shallow place, and you have to know that turtle came in during the night. When it rains in the night, the sand is clean; when it blows in the night, the sand shifts and the cockleburrs get bent; when it really storms, the cottonwoods lose great branches, and those branches rip and crack and peel off strips of bark and tear other limbs as they fall, and they fall into the river. Sometimes a beaver will come along first thing in the morning after a storm and eat those most tender twigs that the night before were a hundred feet high. When the cottonwoods break, then there are holes started in those trees, holes that some birds must have. Then you can think of this river only in terms of its nesting places, cottonwood holes, and wonder just how many cottonwood holes there are along this river for five hundred miles, how many places for a titmouse to nest, how many places for a wild starling, a tree swallow. Cottonwoods and willows, mostly small willows, willows to make a whistle out of, yearling willows, whole populations of willows destined for only a year of life before some torrent carries them down to the ocean with our sand—those are the trees of the Platte.

Not much traffic over a bridge at night, at three, three-thirty in the morning. Not much noise in the air, no convertible with tape-deck blaring, no combines or tractors, no airplanes, no motorcycles, just the dark and the wind and the water moving, making small sounds, and the cottonwood leaves, moving, slippery, talking back to the water. Yes, you can hear the trees out there talking to the water during the night; it's a soft dignified conversation of an old old man with himself, of two old old Indian Chiefs, Chief Cottonwood and Chief Channel, talking slowly and easily late into the night about the times they had together as young ones. The Channel watched the Cottonwoods grow and reminds them of it; but then the Cottonwoods watched the Channel change, get moody, rambunctious, shift positions, and the Cottonwoods remind the Channel of what the trees have seen and they both have a gentle laugh over it all.

You can hear the night insects in the fall, at three-thirty in the morning, when the dew is still forming and there is no wind. From off in the grass comes the insect sound, night insects calling

whirring whistling rattling their wings and legs, and you can close
your eyes and watch the parade of night insects, strutting,
prancing, some walking slowly dragging long antennas, others in a
hurry, turning back from time to time to look along the paths
they've already been, some in halting steps, some in short runs
followed by pauses and whirring of night insects.

They can't hear one another, only their own kinds. Out of all
that symphony they hear only one set of frequencies and ampli-
tudes, call patterns, and they're out there calling to one another,
looking for romance, looking for mates, notifying others of their
presence, telling the world they're out there in the dark wet grass
waiting for something else that lives in the tall wet grass. There are
calls of loneliness. There are calls of old age, of youth. There are
great green ones with long filament antennae out there hidden away
so much in the grass, and while they're hidden and invisible, they
don't want to be invisible so they call and call and whir around with
their legs and wings. But there is one out there that is not like the
rest, and he hears some other species and realizes he is in the middle
of a symphony so he rushes around all through the grass telling the
others to listen to one another. But they can't hear, and they think
he's crazy, and they keep kicking him with their long spiny legs,
until he gives up and goes off to some little place in the grass and
makes his own sound, and listens to all those other sounds, and
finally in some kind of desperation takes his little insect jaws and
nibbles the instructions for re-creating that symphony all along a
piece of Johnson Grass leaf.

And in your dream he keeps nibbling those patterns into that
grass leaf and wanders off looking and listening, and all he sees the
rest of his life are fuzzy out-of-focus patterns of wet grass, and all he
hears now are the symphony sounds of all kinds of insects and birds,
and he keeps nibbling those patterns in the grass leaves until at last
some master scholar bug comes along and finds those patterns, and
starts reading them, and plays a symphony that all the other bugs
can hear, and finally they *all* realize what they've been missing all
this time, and just before the first frost they get together on
purpose and play a last final concert. All because one cricket heard
things that no one else heard. And you must know that when you're
that cricket, then you have learned something of the Platte.

Dawn comes then, after such a pre-dawn darkness, and it's a Joseph Mallord William Turner morning. A person can usually see for many miles on the plains in the morning, and on a Turner morning the spectrum of natural forces is spread out in all directions. The night has been muggy, and a muggy night portends isolated thunderstorms for the day, isolated and scattered thunderstorms, a "band of thunderstorms" extending from one prairie town to another and reported on radar in some city at the other end of the state. There is a smell that blows across the prairie after a muggy night, rolls along with the scattered thunderstorms, pushed into every physical niche of a cottonwood brushline with a plains river hidden below. The smell is clean dirt, gravel road, pickup exhaust, and the weight of the world's grasses, wet from night condensation, wet with temporary violence from isolated thunderstorms, extracted by radiation now coming gray over the land, clearing the mental way for an explosion of reds and oranges and yellows, swirling sky-filled patterns, clouds reflecting colors no one knew existed, the pounding of teal wings high overhead, very high, the last call of the redwing, and the resigned wooden and rusty metal periodic creaking of a windmill water well over in the next section. Morning comes to the east with a domineering supernova of red, and you smile in the normal way you do every morning of your life when the day enters with such force right over the top of some farmstead miles to the horizon, with tall trees and a barn across a green land now reflecting every warm color. It's raining hard in the east, the gray rain forms sheets from the bottom of a flat black cloud that goes for a few miles then stops at the edge of total sunshine, and you can smell the rain hitting the dirt between wiry grass, and you can feel that rain streaking your hair and softening your leather belt, but the brass buckle, the one with the eagle head, never changes with the rain.

Morning comes to the north and it's nothing but a uniform gray fog scudding across the land. The fog will be "burned off," as they say, by noon or two o'clock. Morning comes to the west, and there's a broad place in the west where the deep blues and blue greens refuse to break for the radiation, and you know in your heart that it's hailing in those places. Morning comes to the south, and alone of all the directions the south is the friend of the east and takes the east's colors, spreads them, dilutes them and passes them around to cumulus clouds and wispy clouds, showers and dry grass, the river's string of tall trees winding down along the interstate to the south, winding across the land to the Big Missouri, winding along by a superhighway where a lady from California looks out her window, having just eaten one egg "over easy" and dry toast at a motel in a place called Kearney, and thinks that the prairie river is interesting. But she never wants to go out there and wade in it!

But you can take your simple tools of the biologist's trade, the pan and seine, and wade that river, and you can pan the river for gold, for the gold of knowledge, impressions, feelings, values. And you can seine that river for understanding, you can catch it by the hundreds up in some small pools, and when you've caught it then you'll have caught the understanding of who lives where and in what sizes and in what numbers and with which neighbors, which competitors, which predators, and when it's all over, you will have analyzed in your own way the differences between adjacent twigs, between adjacent rocks, adjacent pools, running water and still water, clear water and sandy water, and water that somehow has slipped beneath a dam, water in oxbows, stagnant water, and water you wouldn't mind to drink. When it's all over, you will have taken your simple tools of the trade and applied them to a five-hundred-mile-long snake, an energy-requiring, energy-transforming machine, with intricate interconnected and interdependent parts. And the fact that your tools as simple as pliers and screwdriver cannot and *will not* do your work for you means that you must use your total mind to understand the river, to discover the essential relationship between its parts, and the fact that the tools will not do your work for you means you must form those impressions that allow you to see, to understand, to appreciate the importance of the river-machine and even the most seemingly minor of its parts. Even the yellowlegs.

And then down along the river in a small town there is a small, old wooden building. Inside, there are the heads of jackrabbits on the wall, and stuck on the heads of those jackrabbits are the antlers of small deer. When you see those things on the wall of such a small wooden building, you don't need to be told what to expect right alongside those rabbit heads: beer signs, maybe issued back in

1963, and posters proclaiming last year's county rodeo, or maybe a motocross, and one with last year's high-school football schedule and scores. And when you see such a place, you don't need to be told what you'll find sitting at the bar: he's large and old, too, and very worn, and two fingers are missing from one hand, and he has every sign of a retired railroad man, including a draught beer and a shot glass with Cabin Still. But what you don't know is that on any Sunday he'll tell you a story of how that river can steal a heart. At least as long as it's a wild river, he'll say, it can steal your heart; but then he'll complain about the canals and dams they've built, never knowing any more than you do who "they" are. You will leave that place with the knowledge that there *are* people out there along the Platte that maybe have applied some simple tools of some trade to their road of the pioneers and have come away with their own kinds of understanding.

So you will wander that river for days, after your talk with that old man, after sharing his beer in that little wooden building, wondering what it is about this river that can occupy the hearts and minds of those who live along it, and your days along the river with your most simple tools of the naturalist's trade will convince you that there is no single part of that river that is not absolutely essential, not even the yellowlegs. They must all be there—all the insects, all the fishes, all the snails, all the spiders spinning those orbs up under overhanging limbs—all of them must be there before the river is wild, before it can steal an old man's heart. But in those places where the river has been dammed, diverted to the servile role, sent out to help till those fields of corn for which these plains are so famous, some parts are missing. So you go back downstream, retracing steps so laboriously pegged out against shifting sands, until you find all those parts in perfect alliance, a river-machine in fine tune, and then it will come as no surprise to you that the river itself upon which you first find that unbanded small flock of three yellowlegs is no different from those birds themselves. Both return from their migrations. But maybe with diminished wild spirits? Perhaps in the case of a river, that giant machine can be chipped away at until it disappears piece by piece into servitude which forever cancels its usefulness as an avenue to the future. Never the bird, however; the bird never is tamed. It's all or none for the yellowlegs.

There is a monumental symbol of servitude out west of here, out where I first walked those dunes with miles of crystal waters over to my left. That monument to servitude is seven miles long, hundreds of feet high, a quarter-mile thick, laid out across the prairies by men working their ways out of a Great Depression. They had no idea what they were doing at the time, that I am sure of; they had no idea they were putting a living river out of the Pleistocene into the service of mankind, but they did it nevertheless. There is a trickle of a stream below that monument to servitude, and it was in that stream that I first learned of the ability of a single element, a single environmental factor, to determine the ability of a larger environment to support life.

That stream is one of those streams that comes from beneath the earthen mountain dam, from way below the earth through an artificial passage buried in the rocks below that ridge of sandy soil. It takes no great knowledge or intelligence to ask about that stream, it's so straight and obviously man-made. It comes from beneath, at the foot of that dam, and it takes no great imagination to believe that its water is that seeping through the soil of that dam's feet. As all this dawns on you, even standing still in that most bitter cold of little streams, you cannot stop the shivers, and your eyes move slowly up that mountain, almost pleading with that structure to stay intact just one more day! That whole panorama of engineering marvel passes before your eyes at times like these, for you know buried down in some file somewhere is the basis for a decision to drain the foot of this dam that holds twenty miles of water above your head. But while your head spins with visions of that decision, wondering if it really was the correct one, your feet turn to stone in water from the bowels of the earth, for that water is the coldest of all upon the Plains. There are some insects that live in that water; you can always see them at your feet. They are larval insects, of the family Simuliidae, of little interest to anyone in this country except those who have seen them and learned of them. They must have oxygen or they will die. There is a place in that little stream from below the dam, a place where there is no oxygen.

But then there is also a place where there *is* oxygen. That place is on the other side of a rock. The larvae live on one side of that rock, and you don't need to be told which side! The single chemical element, the single factor, missing from that water destroys that water's ability to support those flies. The water comes from beneath the dam, from a drain a hundred feet below the hulls of fishing boats, and such water has no oxygen. Until it crosses the rock, that is, such water has no oxygen. How many times in years past I have looked at that single rock, wondering exactly what it was trying to tell me! And how successful my education in ecology along the Platte after sandpipers that I was once a year ago finally able to see the story of that single rock in that single stream. Somewhere there is a single element that must now be in my environment before that niche is suitable for human habitation. That single element flies the night skies with a silver aluminum ankle bracelet, and that single element raised a single chick in the wilds of Keewatin and that single element was, a year ago, waiting for me at the upper end of that great lake held back by that monument to riverine servitude. I knew then there was a rock somewhere to cross. I was days from discovering that rock was the Kansas border!

The first damped rumble of prairie thunder, miles and miles away, spilled over that earthen mountain. One can never tell the real distance of prairie thunder, almost controlled, insistent, soft thunder, no more than one can ever tell the true distance of an owl far off in the woods. But the wind tells, and it then came across the top of that dam and said to hurry, *hurry,* with increasing and directed fingers of the first clouds of fall pointing to the tops of tall cottonwoods able to catch the fingers of a prairie wind jabbing over an earthen mountain. *Hurry,* said the wind, and hurry I did a year ago, for when the prairie wind jabs cloud fingers of fall, then that is warning enough that the spit of winter will come, too, and no migratory animal stays long when that warning is blown. The wind whipped bluestem then, and you must know that one of the indicators of this country is bluestem. When the wind first tells the distance of thunder, when the cloud fingers of fall come over an earthen mountain, hissing a warning through the tops of cottonwoods, then you've been told to take shelter. But when the wind whips bluestem, there are concussions that sound across the prairies, and that is the wind's way of telling you it is serious. No one ignores the wind; I took shelter then. In retrospect it is so obvious that I took shelter then. But the shelter I took was only the shelter of a yellowlegs' wing, the safety of migration, and the shelter of barren mudflats further into the teeth of a storm.

Into the green clouds, across an infinite sea of grass and sand, along that black line of asphalt laid out over the dunes, parallel to the railroad, west into the green gape of hail clouds, the blowing sand of a Great Depression, I took shelter then, across cattle guards scornful of alignments done in town, down rutted roads, ball joint twisting ruts snaking turning back on themselves across a prairie, furtive cattle trails, always west, west into the dark, I took shelter. Into the pools of green slime, stomping through backwater brush through mud and shotgun shells fired a year ago at some goose too high to be bothered, through the capillaries of the upper end of a servile lake, through the plum thickets and year-old willows, I sought shelter out on the flats, the most barren and unprotected of places, with mud and dust combined now in a swirling storm of wind, as lightning hit close and the concussion pumped across the flats and the first of a trillion trillion pieces of rain hit the dirt at the edge of the mud. On the flats stood the critical element!

Wind blew the bird then, and through binoculars with lenses spattered with dusty rain, I could see the feathers lift then return, I could see the head turn this way and that, avoiding the sand blast moving with the speed of a freight across the flats, I could see the wings test themselves, the legs impatient, irritated with the feel of earth, ready for the prairie wind blowing through the toes; *and I could see the thing was banded! Banded! It takes your breath away to see it banded!*

I can be a very competitive son of a bitch when the occasion demands. Someone had handled my childhood dream. Someone had established a so temporary relationship with my symbol of wilderness, but that relationship was closer than mine. Someone had touched a living wild yellowlegs sometime in the past, had marked that event with the anklet, and had released that creature again into the wind. That person had in his mind—for all I know it could have been a *her* mind—a link with the wilderness of this planet that so few others have: a personal band on a wild thing released, a band carried on the wind to the far ends of the earth, along routes no human could take, across places humans could not walk or drive, and at some speed one could never measure! No one has a closer tie with my personal symbol of wilderness, my personal symbol of wild earth-machine in fine tune, than I—no one! Else what's the use of becoming an ecologist? What effect those days on the river must have had on one human psyche that something so simple as a bird band, an aluminum ankle bracelet, could bring out those feelings. I had taken the first steps upon my rock, out there on the flats in the teeth of a prairie storm, and now only to cross the line into that unique econiche wherein one found the single critical element that allows life!

Rain lashed then, pelting torrent, thunder coming upon thunder, with the first storm of fall and the warnings of winter on the river, when nature does things before humans are ready, when nature lives before humans think it should, when every tree on that river does spring while humans seek fire, when a person can stand frozen and see a wild starling carrying food in its mouth. I held binoculars to the bird, my eyes piercing her heart, my own will to go home being sapped and drained into desire to achieve that knowledge, that understanding, of a person who would band a sandpiper. My better judgment crumbled in the heat of desire to fly with this animal, to go, arrow bullet across the wastelands to a place called Argentina, but the yellowlegs moved further out on the mud. I moved with her and still she moved further out, closer to the water, landing far out, almost beyond binocular vision, so far out on the flats.

As quickly as it had come, the prairie storm began to pass, and the rain that had driven itself and the dust and sand before it now breathed more slowly, steadily, smaller droplets. But the wind shifted then, turning from the hills to the north, and I knew that before I would see my river again that rain would have turned to sleet and ice would cover the land many feet deep and there would be many miles on worn ecologists and tired birds. It was time then;

66

the gray wings lifted and she was gone, gone into the southern horizon, and I followed. It is just as simple as that. I do remember casting aside the simple pan and net of my trade; those are the things with which to see bugs and fish.

And I do remember those first steps out on the mudflats south, south to the line across which my single critical element had flown.

Part II
THE TRIP

8 ᔕ Kansas

*Lured on by tales of rich lands, where kings were supposed
to be lulled to sleep by the chimes of golden bells,
Coronado eventually reached Kansas . . .*

Peter Farb

*I*t had been covered by ocean once, many millions of years
back when the great reptiles' history was coming to an end. And on
the shores of that ocean had evolved and lived out *its* history a
magnificent creature *Hesperornis,* loon-like giant flightless bird,
plowing the gulf for fishes never to be seen by man except in rocken
memory. One can visualize that great fishing bird easily if one has
held a duck, a penguin, or wounded heron; *Hesperornis* is strong,
strong as steel and wire, and quick, quick enough below the surface
to snap those fish of the murky brine blown against that which
would eventually be the Flint Hills; and *Hesperornis* is primitive and
old; and if asked, *Hesperornis* would reply with its eyes that this had
always been ocean (after all, had it not been ocean long enough for
such a life form to evolve?) and always would be ocean forever and
ever. But *Hesperornis* was not the first nor the last living thing to
believe something about its own environment that turned out not
to be true!

It had been covered by tall grass once, once many thousands of
years back when the age of innocence was beginning to end, and
upon the tall grass and around the outcrops there moved in silence
of early fall, the searing heat of what would come to be called

"July," the marching drifts of what would later be known as "January," the great herds of classic herbivores. It was a passive and forbearant role that these warm giants played, and it was the same role which had been played since soon after life crept out of the Devonian puddles onto the land, played by the dinosaur with forehead horns and bony shields to cover a vulnerable neck. The face of such a land as we now know it was essentially established by the time of warm herds, and they wallowed in places, and made more places, and pawed the earth below rich grass until the dirt blew, and nuzzled and suckled their wobbly calves and ducked their horns at watchful wolves and coyotes and lived out the endless endless times looking as far as their small eyes could see out over an ocean of their own kind. And if asked, these bison would say yes the prairie had always been here and would always be here, as would the herds that every *bison* knew ruled the land as far as the small eye could see, only slightly conceding that the plains might also have room for coyotes and even lesser creatures such as golden mosquitoes and a gray bird that waded up to its belly in the mud of a wallow following the September storm, skimmed the beetles off the surface. Then it waded out only to its bright yellow ankles before unslotted primaries and a faired trailing edge took that creature so rapidly across the land that a bison could not understand. The bird flickered in the beast's vision, gaze fixed on several blades of prairie grass, and was gone.

The beast itself was soon to flicker in the vision of this land and was soon itself to be virtually gone. But one day there stood in the willows of an intermittent stream, designed to direct the flow of only occasional rainwater into a sand and gravel river miles away, a half-naked and filthy man with a shaft in his hand. Fixed to the end of that shaft was what some person in the age of machinery would call a Folsum Point, and marvel at the workmanship soon to be jammed between the ribs of great bison, and wonder what the maker of that point could do with a modern metal lathe. The man had stood for a long time watching the herd, substituting his brain's work for the brawn that had served so many other predators so well. The man and his prey marched the same road of time through the Flint Hills. A few of both would remain in museums in the form of pitted skulls and reconstructions.

The smaller bison that would replace his target was still in a future so distant this scraggy fellow could never feel or know or sense, but it, too, would feel the sting of a technological advancement, multiplying not only the predator power of this helpless migratory ape, but more importantly his options for further multiplications of predator power through the application of combinations and permutations. For in the technicon known as human brain, even the most simple idea provided raw material for numerous other ideas, each combination of old ideas, elaborations of old ideas plus combinations of old ideas, plus combinations of combinations which were in themselves new ideas—all suddenly grown complicated and sophisticated. He may have died at an early age, but he was cunning and crafty and a dreamer and resourceful, so that when a Spanish galleon landed, dropped a plank onto the New World, and led some things called horses down that plank, when that first hoof clomped down on the soil of America, wiry Indian might well have looked through those same willows and stated in flowing natural words "one small step for horse, one giant step for Indian." A new machine, marvelously coordinated with feedback informational flow and servomechanisms, ghosted across a prairie with all the beauty and speed that a poor woman with worn moccasins and aching low legs and back could visualize. So her man caught and stole and raised that new machine, and if he was smart enough through heritage, he then tamed it, rode it against the buffalo, and exploited it in any of hundreds of the most imaginative and creative ways any thing called human had or would have exploited a technicon. If he were heritage poor, he would instead eat the new machine, lacking the creativity of his brothers now riding high with eagle feathers and friends.

They had no way of knowing, these creative savages, on the second of May in the year of 1803 when Francois de Barbé-Marbois scrawled his signature across a bit of parchment then pushed it across the table to James Monroe, that the sea of bison and grass upon which they played with their new machine, wild horses, *mesteños,* had just been bought and sold by a couple of types they never imagined existed. The cultural distance was every bit as great as if the arm of the Milky Way were at this very moment being purchased by some living things engaged in Napoleonic Wars of a nature beyond our imagination, concerned about trade through an avenue of the universe, and on the verge of sending a couple of generals named Lewis and Clark to explore the new territories. It was all coming to an end, and within the lifetimes of brown berries carried on the backs of mothers, there would be the marches, the wagons, the killings and mutilations, the broken promises, the dregs of a Civil War fought over issues the bison hunters could not understand, and the cutting edge of a plow breaking for the first time a soil that never knew a "plow" existed. The grandchildren of those brown berries would stand on the prairies of their ancestors and watch a machine start a hole that would cut through even the time of *Hesperornis* back to the oil- and gas-bearing sands and shales. The grandchildren of those berries would stand and watch a dragster reach a hundred miles an hour within the course of a quarter-mile blacktop then pop a parachute. They would stand out beside a run-down shack and watch a silver bird leave exhaust trails across a blue sky and wonder why they were not able to get a job at the plant that made those things. And one of those great grandchildren would stop wiping the windshield of a large automobile, pulled in beside the yellow pump of a cut-rate gas station in a town where a President was raised, and look across the four-lane street and wonder who in the hell was that guy drag-assing along under the interstate bridge in jeans with mud up to the knees and a field jacket that still dripped with the morning's rain.

Tall Kiowa had swooped out of the Flint Hills along this same trail, feathers blowing with manes and tails of hunting party. Tall Comanche had thundered in packs hanging by a fistful of hair from the back of a pony scarcely more wild than its owner and temporary master in and out of gullies and cottonwoods, spears and later rifles adorned with feather couplets, spinning on a short string, spinning fast dervish on a small string tied to the end of a muzzle aimed at a settler who probably had no business there other than the replacement of one biotype by another. Tall Kiowa and thundering Comanche were gone, gone into the abyss with *Hesperornis,* but perhaps reconstructed like *Hesperornis* out of evidence for a prior existence. In the place of Kiowa and Comanche, there now zipped along the interstate east and west the product of America, all colors, all fabrics, kid in '63 Chevy, Mickey Thompson tires riding

high rear end headed for a quarter-mile strip in a place called
Newton, grandmother in '64 Galaxy two-door with original paint
and upholstery, a parade of Japanese ingenuity, whining, straining
at the brute bigness of a country that needed an "Interstate
System," Kenworths with yachts for an eastern owner, all blaring
local rock stations, the Bee Gees on stereo tape deck, Lester Flatt
and Earl Scruggs by a DJ out of a place no one knew was there and
could only get with static, the local grain markets reports out of
Kansas City, "breaker one nine" from down the road, the local
weather, news, sports, high school football with an undecided
opponent; dove season, pheasant season coming up, teal flying,
another disastrous four months for the purple and white, a load of
drill pipe, a Hall of Fame for racing dogs, largest Western-wear
store, and amidst the wonder of it all walking college professor,
skipping classes, wet, muddy, tired, binoculars swinging, sunglasses on a cloudy day, south in the southbound lane, an eye
toward the place where a sun was supposed to be, but most
importantly—oh, yes, *most* importantly—between the thumb and
the middle finger of the left hand, pinched in finger vise, no
escape . . .

. . . *a feather from the left breast of a banded lesser yellowlegs!*

It was slightly curled, this feather, but not rigid, not hard in
texture. No, it was a soft feather, elongate, gray-white, with light-
brown, gray-rust markings that were at once the most distinct and
most common. Where had nature gotten such a design, so simple
yet so distinct, a design never repeated on any item of women's
clothing? One could only guess, but it was a design repeated in
myriad subtle forms on feather after feather on bird after bird until
almost everywhere one looked there was that design or some
modification of it. It was a light feather, with a flat fattened
Phoenician-Roman "V," spear of color along the shaft and through
the point, blending into bracket, into the top of a shield, into the
same pattern family, and all its genera and species gracing the
individual feathers of any one species from neck to flank to under
tail coverts. The arrow-bracket, the flying V, was repeated down
the length of a feather from just beneath the wing, a *sandpiper*
feather, picked up on the black shore of a farm pond.

I'd lain in the grass as the heavy misting sky lightened in the east and had focused binoculars on a pockmarked break in the prairie a hundred yards away to learn things about a yellowlegs I'd never known: its feeding style, its head movements, the depth to which it waded, the angle of its leg joints, and the way it stood with one foot resting so slightly upon a lip of cow track and watched the horizon for a moment, turning this way, then directly toward a man in the grass staring at her, whom she watched for what seemed like an unusually long time, before stepping again into the mud. I'd seen the feather fall, preened out with the wing raised, scratched with a foot that probably had snail eggs stuck to it, and I'd held my breath while the bird moved on down the bank. It would not do for that bird to step on such a precious feather! What a decision, whether to go at the very moment and pick it up, risk scaring the bird, maybe sending it far away forever only for the sake of a single feather, or so that it not be picked up by some ant, not be stepped on by a beef steer! In the end I waited. When I awakened, the bird was gone. I was instead in the middle of a herd. They waited in total silence while my eyes focused, watching, breathing heavily, some chewing, all watching, standing, one swinging a massive head around to rub a shoulder, just staring at a man asleep in the grass of Kansas pasture a hundred yards from a pond where a sandpiper had dropped a feather.

I was on familiar territory behaviorally, for although I could easily have been labeled *vagrant* by the conservative young wives pulling out of a grocery store parking lot, uncomfortably locking their car doors when they caught sight of me across the four-lane, I was nevertheless engaged in an activity that had supported me all my adult life: biological research. I was doing biological research for the sole and total personal pleasure of satisfying my own curiosity about a natural-phenomenon-machine-cybernetic-wonder capable of movements and responses so subtle as to be non-detectable by human eyes, as well as movements in response to the turning of a planet or the orbit of that planet about a star. I was doing research on a cybernetic wonder called *Tringa flavipes,* the lesser yellowlegs, and would soon be teaching the results of that research, for the feather now clamped in vice pinch was a blackboard, and my mind was filled with tales of miracles and truths beyond the wildest fiction. Woe be indeed to the first intelligent being to actually encounter this apparition in its frenzied state of thrill over the movements of a sandpiper and the fact of a dropped feather!

Yes, woe indeed! For along with the feather came a sense of responsibility: teach, tell someone of the yellowlegs; tell someone of the things to be seen along the Platte! With only a feather against monolithic ignorance, I would stalk the plains of Midnation, of Kansas! Find that chink in the armor of myopia that refused to see sandpipers on that horizon into the future! Share the thrill of discovery, of original research, with somebody! My mind boiled, as it often does while I travel, or do rote motions for long periods, with the excitement of challenge and the size of the task! Take a feather and explain ecology to Kansas! I could do it! I *would* do it!

"Feather quiz, Pops!"

"Pops" returned the shotgun to its corner, still well within an instant's reach beneath the bar of Merl's family business, Merl's Bar and Grill/Auto Shop/Whore House/Used-Car Sales. He'd gazed through a clear place in a painted window at the figure step-by-stepping it out from under the bridge, and shaken his head to himself. He thought he knew what was coming. These men off the road, they always asked for work, meals, maybe a bottle of wine, never a beer. Some begged outright for money ("travelin' on the road and need money for a bus ticket to Little Rock where my sister's dyin'"). They always smelled of something, and their clothes were always more worn up close than from across the street. But *binoculars?* In all his years at this corner, including those from back in the thirties when even respectable people were out of work and "on the road," none had ever had a pair of *binoculars* slung around his neck!

I wrenched myself up on a stool and leaned with aching back over the vinyl edge of the bar itself. My eyes were still not adjusted to the light, but in the reddish glow I could see the old man standing to the left of an ancient cash register. The place reeked of stale beer, popcorn, automobile exhaust, transmission fluid, spray paint and cheap perfume. The sun broke through briefly, as it often does on the central plains after a morning rain, clouds parting slightly, portending a great day, drying puddles. I held the feather with a vise grip by the shaft, hand on the bar, and a look of total reverence, serene reverence, must have passed over my face. The old man noticed and became very alert, wary. The breaking sun sent a stray shaft through the clear place on a painted prairie bar window and that stray shaft fell upon the feather, bathing it in an unearthly and eerie light with cigaret smoke, as I turned it around and around, still serene, still wet, and still an ecologist.

"Species and part of body?"

Pops looked for a long time at the feather, the man off the highway, then back again at the feather. He finally took it gently, holding it in the light for a moment, turning it over and over, holding it back in the shaft of light, holding it over under the bulb by the cash register, flattening it against his palm, holding it up to the window to look through, and at last smiling.

"That's a yellowshanks feather," he said, "come off up by the wing." He gently handed the feather back. "I cleaned many o' them birds back years ago, probably back before you's born, used to shoot 'em by the hundreds, right along with ducks and geese. 'Specially down at the marshes where Great Bend is, yellowshanks used to come into those marshes by the millions. Shoot a truckload if'n a guy wanted!"

And the old man then began a tale the likes of which I hope never again to hear; a tale of naïveté in an age of ignorance; a tale of blood and thunder; a tale of consumption and wanton waste; a tale of earth products tasted but never to be tasted again; a tale of blunted sensitivities and Machiavellian practicality; a tale of the hunting of gray bullet cybernetic machine highly coordinated energy budgeting shapely head and neck lesser yellowlegs; a tale of hunting the marshes of a great sink hole called the Bottoms.

"There is a place down by Great Bend," he began, "where we used to go many years ago. Wasn't much down in this country then, few farms and ranches, and I come down from Box Butte County up in Nebraska with my own folks. Mother was took sick on the way. Settled in down by Salina, or at least where Salina is now. That old house is still standin', back off the main streets. My sister tells me it's still standin'; sees it once in a while. She lives in Salina, you know that?"

"I didn't know your sister still lived in Salina."

"Yeah, she's still down there, been down there all the time since we's kids. Married some no-good down there; he's dead now, o'course, good riddance. She's a lot better off'n if he's still alive. Had to work all her life just t' take care o' that no-good sumbitch." The old man coughed a few times, turning back to the wall; a dry cough.

"Didn't know your brother-in-law had died."

"Dad used to take me when I's a kid. Ride all day down from Salina in that old wagon just to get to the marshes. Leave early early in the mornin', way before sun's up, get down there late afternoon and start shootin' them birds. Sit up most all night cleanin', throw 'em in the back of that wagon, get up next mornin' start shootin' again, huntin' down all them ducks, geese, them yellowshanks. Clean 'em fast, just rip off the skin and cut off the breasts and throw 'em in the wagon. Got home, o' course, had to salt 'em down, cook 'em up into sausage, do all sorts of stuff. Dry 'em in the smoke house. Sell a bunch to folks around who couldn't make it down to the marshes. Oh, them marshes is a *great* place! I never *ever* seen no place as great as them marshes!" The old man was almost wistful. "I don't think I ever seen *any* place as great as them marshes back when I's a kid."

"Prairie marsh is a great place." I paid for a beer, and it must have surprised the old man. The morning sun grew stronger through the hole in the window paint, and I stared at the single feather now lying on the bar between us.

"Used to go out before daylight and build up a little blind, pull together whatever brush and old cattail stalks you could find. Didn't need much in those days, just throw some stuff together to hide behind and wait for 'em. Oh, they'd come right on in to it every time, come right on in to all that flyin' shot and powder. Sound like a real war out there on the marshes at times. Used to get a bunch from all over the county ride on in to Great Bend and go out to the marshes, shoot up a supply of meat. 'Course the meat wasn't all there was to it. Just gettin' out and bein' in the nature was a lot of it. Oh, you'd get a bunch of meat if the ducks and geese was in and flyin'. Never got much meat off yellowshanks, but sure got lots of pleasure at bein' out on the marshes at daybreak. My dad always loved nature; taught me to enjoy it when I's a kid."

"I can tell that."

"Sometimes it'd be chilly, maybe damp and chilly out there in the mornin' makin' that blind, but when the birds come in you'd forget about all that and just start killin' 'em. They'd come in in a big flock, sometimes great big flock, not a tight flock so's you could kill a bunch with just a couple of shots, mind you, but big anyways. Some folks used decoys. We never used no decoys for them yellowshanks; didn't have to. They's curious birds, social, you could whistle 'em right on in. Better yet, just wait. If your blind's in the right spot, maybe one or two come along, bust 'em. Worked best if they's not killed outright, but just wounded. Flop around there on the mud for a while and attract a bunch more. O' course you had to get out and try to chase 'em. Sometimes if they's just hit in the wing and not in the legs or body, have the damndest time tryin' to catch 'em. Run around, fallin' down, hoppin' up, scuttlin' through the grass all bloody, leavin' blood and feathers out on the mud. Feathers just like this one." The old man picked up the feather again and held it in the shaft of light. "I seen many a feather just like this one out there on the mud, *many* a feather all right!"

"Hit birds out on the mud had the damndest sound, almost a scream. You'd chase 'em around out there slippin' and slidin' all over the place, tryin' to keep clean and dry, and here they'd go off through the grass with that scream of theirs, bleedin' and stumblin', wings draggin', sometimes twisted around way over their backs and all bloody underneath. But they'd sure make the damndest screams like you'd never heard. Almost drive a man crazy if it wasn't for the fact that they'd bring in a bunch more with them screams!" The old man chuckled and shook his head slowly. "Yeah, I tell you for a kid out there in them blinds them screams would sure put the fear into you, except for the others they brought in. Sometimes the old man'd send me out to chase the wounded birds, make 'em scream, run around in the mud for a while, then tell me in a hurry to get back in the blind. That always meant there's a bunch more comin' in. I guess he didn't want to accidentally shoot his own kid when the yellowshanks come in!"

"Guess not." I stared into beer.

"Finally catch 'em, just pull their heads off. Course had to hold 'em down so's the blood wouldn't get all over your pants. Bird blood gets awfully sticky. Have to wear that same pair of pants for a week. Just pull their heads off, that stopped that screamin' right quick. Course by that time we'd always have shot a bunch more, just leave the dead ones out there on the mud, they's your decoys. Didn't need to make decoys; never could figure out why all those rich guys used to have all them carved decoys they'd stick out on the mud. We'd always just kill a few and leave 'em lay. Besides, old man could always whistle just like a yellowshanks. They had a bunch of whistles and I must say, that of all the kids in Salina, I was the one whose dad could do all those whistles. Not only yellowshanks, but a bunch of others. He could do all kinds. He could do a screech owl like you never heard! Sit out in the woods and do a screech owl over and over again, next thing you know the trees is full of little birds all upset over an owl nearby! Used to shoot a bunch of them birds, too. They's hard to hit, some o' them little ones. Used to think they's so small they slipped through the pattern. You know a shotgun makes a pattern a shot."

"I know."

"Actually, get a dead yellowshanks out on the mud and a guy could just whistle in about every bird in miles. All kinds of calls they had. *Pill-e-wee, pill-e-wee, pill-e-wee.*" It was a strange and wild sound the old man made, drifting through the darkened corners of a darkened tavern on the outskirts of middle America. I could feel the mist and chill of a morning back in the 1920s or before, the wrenching jolt of a hard wagon seat over the miles between what is now Salina and some sink hole marshes, the wet cattails thrown into a blind where a boy crouched with his grizzled father from the old country on one side and a shotgun too big for him to handle on the other. "*Pill-e-wee, pill-e-wee, pill-e-wee.*" Low pitched, almost soft but insistent, was that call, that call to gather, an "all's safe" spreading confidence among a weary migrating flock just before that grizzled man, with a twist of his mouth, and that young boy, manly, hoisting big gun, wincing at the recoil but nevertheless manly, rose up out of the cattails to kill and kill and spread the Cheyenne mud with the blood of yellowshanks and feathers with Roman vees speared through on the shaft with a mark.

"*Pill-e-wee, pill-e-wee, pill-e-wee.* Old man could call 'em in skillful as hell. Get a couple on the ground they'd sometimes give just a single whistle, *wheu,* soft, so soft you could hardly hear it, mellow, soft, most gentle little whistle I ever heard out of any game animal. Almost a welcome call it was, *wheu,* wait a few seconds, give another, *wheu,* wait another few seconds, give another, *wheu.* Birds act almost as if they'd found some friends down on the mud, almost as if they'd been told they's *welcome;* that's it, a *welcome* call! They'd drop on out of the sky like you never seen; *welcome,* that's what that little whistle meant, *welcome.* My dad could make that *welcome* call almost perfect. We'd welcome 'em all right!"

"I bet you did."

"Make some other sounds out there, flyin' out over the marshes. Little soft calls, awful soft but you could hear 'em way out over the marshes, *companionship,* that's what my old man used to say those calls were, *companionship* with one another. Held the flock together, those calls. He'd give 'em that call right after we'd blasted away for a while, flock would go back together, circle out over the marshes, then he'd call 'em back in with that yodle and whistle and we'd start in shootin'."

"Don't hunt those birds anymore."

"Shame," said the old man, "can't think of much better way for a boy to get to learn about nature." The old man chuckled to himself and shook his head in that slow way of his. "That's been a long long time back when all that happened. Can't remember the last time we went out, but I's a kid all that time, just a kid. I remember one time just before my mom got real sick, right before she died, went down to them marshes and my dad called in the biggest flock you seen anywhere. We just sort of let 'em come on in 'til they's all down, then let 'em have it right here on the ground. Dad shot one way, I shot the other. Had a contest, see who killed the most."

"Who killed the most?" I asked, almost curious.

"I did. See, I figured I could pull off one barrel then the other, real quick after one another, and get a bunch with the first shot, then another bunch with the second right before they took off. Figured that first shot would scare 'em a little so's they'd raise their wings, then I'd wound a bunch, all in that instant with their wings up."

"Did it work?"

"Oh, you bet! Course I had to do a lot of chasin' and pullin' off

heads to get all mine, Dad just laughin' in the blind watchin' me do
all that runnin', but I sure as hell won the contest!"

"How many?"

"Don't remember for sure, but it was over a hundred. I do
remember it was over a hundred with just them two shots."

"You done real well that day."

"You bet I done real well that day!" said the old man.

"I'm on the road, Pops, need some help gettin' on down south.
What you got on the lot that's worth a shit?"

"*This* lot?"

"This lot, yours, the one right out there, 'Used Car Sales,' it
says."

"Never sold no cars off that lot!" said the old man behind the
bar.

"*Never sold a used car?*"

"Started that part up about a year ago. Ain't sold nothin' yet! Do
all right on chicken fried steak. Get you a girl without much
trouble. Knock a dent out in the gee-rage, put on a new water
pump, air cleaner, overhaul a rear end once in a while. Never sold
none o' them cars in the year they's been sittin' out there."

"Got anything worth a shit out there?"

"You got any money, son?"

"I got *good American* money."

"Ain't that the only kind they is?"

"Give me the keys to the old Mustang." Someplace back in the
back of the bar the old man fumbled in a drawer, then fumbled
around in another drawer, and came up with three sets of Ford keys,
all about the same year as a late sixties worn-paint white Mustang
with black stripe sitting now under a signpost with leftover sparrow
nests and rotting electrical wiring, a white Mustang with grass
uncut beneath it.

"I *think* one of these sets goes to the Mustang. You plannin' to
drive?"

"That I am, Pops!"

"You got any identification of any kind, driver's license,
anything of value? You know some guy come in off the road, I can't
just give some guy off the road the keys to one of my cars. You
know that, son, right?"

"If it runs all right, I'll buy it; cash. In the meantime, you hang on to that feather. I'll get it back when I bring your car back."

"You leavin' a feather so's I can make sure you ain't runnin' off with my used car?!"

"That's right, Pops." I gently lifted one of the three sets of keys out of his hand. "And you better damn well make sure it's still there when I get back."

"No one never put no kind of value on a yellowshanks feather!"

"You may start now."

I stood before the worn machinery, and all of my technological society passed before my eyes. There in powdery white baked enamel was a designer's dream, a predatory act upon the psyche of an affluent technicon-dependent population of ingenious people who admired the even more ingenious. There in white enamel sat a designer's predatory act which correctly assumed that the machinery age had dulled America's sense of machinery, that a technological level had been reached in which people always assumed machines worked properly, thus never questioned the interrelations of parts. Or else these Americans assumed the interrelations of parts too complicated a subject of the machine age. So these innocents chose machines instead upon the way they *looked,* but still without knowing what to look *for!* Ah, for a Master Mechanic who knew no matter what the machine, the things to look *for* would reveal the interrelations of parts, the attitudes of previous owners! Perhaps those things to look *for* were universal, I thought, standing on Kansas fall grass. Perhaps some sense, even a sense of the river on a Turner morning, even a sense of that willowy call from the darkness above, was the sense that allowed one to see the attitudes of previous owners. The educated romantic—was that the key, was that the approach one needed now at a moment of decision? So Pops stood at the door of a prairie bar, feather held tightly between thumb and forefinger, and watched the educated romantic, a man he did not know was a distinguished *scientist,* start a used Mustang time after time, reaching through the front window, never touching the gas, and listening, simply listening, to lowgrowl engine now awake after nearly a year at Merl's Bar and Grill.

The odometer read 98674.3 miles. The gas gauge showed a quarter tank. The smell of vinyl saturated the inside. The sum total workings shuddered slightly down the block but smoothed into an almost migratory feel within a mile, and outside of town I slowly pushed the pedal to the floor, and the machine obeyed and went a hundred miles an hour. I turned around in a gravel driveway past a section line road and returned to Pops' place past a row of graceful mansions one never expected to find in a prairie town.

"I'll take it. Here's your money. Give me my feather."

"That's not enough."

"That's all you get, Pops."

"Then I'm keepin' the feather." His eyes were wide, as if the challenge of a younger man 'off the road' were not a thing Pops had ever tried before. "Pay me the other two hundred or I'm keepin' the feather."

"Keep the feather. Sell it to someone else for two hundred dollars; tell 'em about gettin' to know the nature out in the Bottoms. Then tell 'em no one has contests anymore to see who can kill the most yellowlegs. Tell 'em about the screams out on the mud. Then tell 'em some guy come in off the road sixty years later with a two-hundred-dollar feather and show 'em the feather. Yeah, Pops, show 'em the feather. But don't sell it for less than the full two hundred. Show 'em what kind of value you and I put on that feather."

No need to ask, of course. Pops knew the younger man was headed for the Bottoms. Migratory animals always headed for the Bottoms, just as they always headed for the few other major staging areas along a prairie route to a place called South America. Hops, several-hundred-mile hops, from one vast marsh to another—that's what migratory animals did. Pops still held the single feather, pinched by the shaft between thumb and forefinger, a two-hundred-dollar feather. He shook off the feeling that it had maybe come off the man rather than the bird. The feather would be good but not for the full two hundred, not for hard cash, but for the kind of life support that often hard cash could not buy in a prairie town for an old man running the family business to the end of his days. Such life support took the form of a tale, best of all a true tale, the tale of wonder. He held such a tale, and toward the end of the day there would be cronies with whom to share it! And there was proof upon proof; *the* feather, stowed carefully now beneath the tray of his cash register, in the same place he would stow the *big* checks if anyone had ever written any checks in his business; *the* place where the Mustang had been, the uncut grass, a touch of dark petroleum which, all things considered, was not much for a year's worth of drippings; but as much as anything, an accomplice down at the bank.

"Ask Elmer's boy down at the bank," Pops would say later that afternoon. "Had him check 'em all. Took 'em back into the back room with that other kid just moved down here from Clay Center. New hundreds, they was, brand new with numbers in order."

"New kid moved down here from Clay Center and moved into the old Ruder house." The speaker was heavy, his gnarled hands missed two fingers on the left. These cronies through all these places, they were all the same, and if not the same, then of the same mold.

"Never knew where they moved," said Pops. "Just knew they moved down from Clay Center not too long after the storm." "The Storm" had ripped roofs and facings from houses and churches, leaving full-sized doll houses, furniture exposed, with full-sized dolls walking numb among the rubble looking for family pictures. "The Storm" had uprooted full-grown elm trees around a band shell in the Public Park, and "The Storm" had twisted windmills into balls of angle iron that still lay, like dead and contorted insects, in overgrazed pastures. "Anyway, Elmer's boy told me they's real. Looked 'em over real good, he and that other kid. Don't get brand new hundreds too often from some guy off the road."

"You don't get brand new hundreds too often from *any*body, Pops. Hell, I believe you. Sell one car in a year. Keep a strange feather in your cash register. Goin' crazy, Pops, that's what you are, goin' crazy." But of course he would find a way to check out the story about the new bills. And he had to admit that for the first time in many such days and weeks, there *was* a glow about Pops' place, a glow he could not exactly explain, but nevertheless a glow of sorts. A somewhat vitalized Pops, perhaps? It was almost as if something had come up out of Pops' youth, something like a time remembered, activities remembered, things of value, but things viewed in the new perspective of a life behind the bar of a small city amidst a sea of grass. So he decided to stay later today. His wife was

also a large woman, and their daily meal of potatoes and a roast off
the steer he'd butchered last March would wait: she stoic, the meal
cold but no worse cold than hot, the gravy jellied. "Gimmie
another, Pops. Yep, goin' crazy. Must have been some guy off the
road, make you do all those things, keepin' a feather in the cash
register. Made you go crazy, Pops, that's what he did."

Pops held a curved glass at an angle so the tap would not make a
head, lip of the glass right up touching the spigot, and he ran the
beer all the way to the rim. From a special bottle of cheap blended
something-or-other, he filled the shot glass beside the draught.
They talked for a long time about the young man off the road,
about what he actually was doing in this town, how a young man
like that could just go from place to place without no work but
with some money in a brown envelope and a pair of *binoculars* slung
around his neck, how he'd wanted to know all about Pops' younger
days when they hunted the yellowshanks, and how maybe Pops
wished he hadn't killed quite so many of those birds in his few short
years as an innocent lad. They took the feather out from beneath the
cash tray and looked it over again, and before long a woman and a
man came in, she bursting the seams of black gabardine slacks and
swinging a large purse, he wiry, thin, stooped slightly, with green
coveralls, lace-up boots and a billed cap with mesh on the back and
a Texaco emblem on the front. So the story of the young man who
bought the first used car in a year and left some large bills as well as
a feather that Pops kept in the cash register had to be told again. It
was told again when Dean come in from the shop, wiping hands,
sitting down at his usual place at the end of the bar and the end of
the day. It was told again when Rosie come in from the motel, all
ready for work. It was told again down at the T.G.&Y. store and
again down in the Rexall Drug. A young man who had just
graduated from the University of Missouri School of Journalism and
worked on his first job at the paper heard about it and interviewed
Pops; but when the story finally appeared, it was only three
paragraphs back behind the sports page.

But out beside Highway 15, off on the shoulder and in the bar
ditch where a tall and tanned man with pressed work shirt stood
mending a fence after a rain, four-wheel-drive new pickup beside
him in the ditch, empty gun rack in the back window, ever-present

mesh cap with adjustable plastic band across the back, the story lingered as did the sandpipers in the rain pool a hundred yards away. The man lingered also, resting his arm on the wooden fence post, resting his claw hammer, watching the birds, thinking about the strange story, wondering why he had never really watched those birds before, deciding they were pretty and graceful, wishing his wife were here to see them. He stopped again a time or two before the mending job was done. When he stepped high back into the cab, tossing the hammer on the passenger's side of the seat, he smiled. It had been a good day. It had been a good year and a good season. His pickup was paid for, and he and his wife were both healthy and in their primes. Their second kid would be starting to college next year and with a little luck, she would go on a track scholarship. Their first had just finished the Kansas City Art Institute and had moved to New Mexico where he sold things for more money than the man in the pickup had ever seen as a youth. Their "baby" would be in junior high, and he alone of the three seemed destined for the ranch and the family property. The man guided the pickup home, leaving a sweeping pair of muddy tracks along Highway 15, blobs spattering the inside of fenders for a quarter mile. He would bring the youngest out with him next time. A boy who would take over the family land should probably see the sandpipers around a rain puddle.

9 ➣ The Bottoms

In the wind are pungent odors from
the marshes by the road.
Robert M. Pirsig

*T*hey had argued in the older days, these older men, as to exactly where from came the Bottoms. "Sink hole," some had called the Bottoms, conjuring up an event in which the floor of the prairie gave way and the land dropped, dropped some more, filled with water for fifty or a hundred square miles, grew cattails and sedges if there *were* cattails and sedges when all this happened, and served as a nesting ground for untold millions of water birds if there *were* water birds when all this happened. The sink in the prairie was a convenient day's flight from the Great Salt Plains in the state to the south. It was a convenient few hours at most from Merl's Bar and Grill for a person in a white Mustang with a black stripe. It was a convenient few hours from most places where a Game Commissioner could get into a large green car and drive to his favorite marshes to see firsthand the results of his latest "management" scheme. It was a convenient few minutes' walk from the nearest hollow cottonwood or cut under bank for the average raccoon or skunk when the Commissioner's "management" scheme laid bare thousands of teal nests as part of the marsh was drained, *on purpose*. It was a convenient few seconds away from uncountable millions of floodwater mosquitoes that rested on grasses and awaited the passing cow, human, dog, roosting meadowlark. And as far as the eye could see, there was beneath the grass moist mud. Those mosquitoes would lay eggs on that moist soil, eggs that would spend the winter as dust only to explode again in June rains into more uncountable millions of floodwater mosquitoes.

The Bottoms was a convenient home for thousands of crows and gulls that gleaned the carrion of a "managed" marsh. It was a convenient resting place for a white pelican to eat so many carp it was unable to fly, there to be captured by a cowboy in an airboat and given to the zoo, which in turn traded it for something more exciting than a pelican. Plains residents had seen pelicans before. And the Bottoms had all been made more convenient by a series of dikes, topped by roads and pierced by gates, that ran through the marshes and divided the sink hole into "ponds" which could be independently drained, planted in millet, or cleaned of carp, i.e., pelican food. A sink-hole marsh had been turned into a machine that could be driven by management convinced it could drive it better than its original owners. I sat in the old white car out on a dike road with only marsh as far as I could see, except for the rim of the sink hole miles to the horizon, and searched the flats and sloughs for a single banded bird. It was a simple activity, this search. To sit in a car and look at the water with binoculars was one of the oldest tricks of the trade, and it was guaranteed, same as that stroll along the Platte which seemed so long ago to produce the required mental state.

A marsh was an exponential function, and that fact was probably the one that should have been made most clearly to anyone who ever tried to tamper with one. Quality plotted on a vertical log scale against area plotted on a horizontal linear scale would have produced a straight line. Stated more simply, a large marsh was not only a large version of a small marsh; no, the character and richness of a marsh grew disproportionately with its size. A large marsh was *more* than the sum of small marshes. Still staring with binoculars from the dike road, I wondered if anyone had ever considered that fact when someone decided to make this large marsh into several small ones so the whole thing could be "managed." Somewhere in the back of my mind was an idea that life was like this also. The whole of a living thing was always more than the sum of its parts. Even a human life, that also was more than the sum of its parts, and

I wondered even then about the division of a human life or a marsh into smaller ones so something could be managed. I wondered even then of those exponential qualities that might be lost through the construction of dikes and draining of the ponds of a human time on earth. But the Bottoms that day was alive, as alive as any organism!

The assemblages in the air over fifty or a hundred square miles of marsh need to be seen, not described. The sky rotates above a prairie marsh, especially in Indian Summer, when the sky above takes command from the water and rushes below, takes command of the attention. It's this way and that for a boy with binocs in an old car out on the dikes, and the panorama of movement swirls with majestic turns in the distance, casual formations of gulls, serious purposeful heavy lines of geese, hurtling flying saucer knots of teal, flashing underwings of sanderlings in perfect coordination and harmony motion, the forced but graceful flight of a bittern in the distance, all accented as always by piercing commentary from a lone killdeer. And in a slough where a bar ditch runs out, a line of dowitchers does what dowitcher does best: sleeps with bill under wing. And besides a line of sleeping dowitchers is a banded female lesser yellowlegs sweeping beetles from the surface of a hundred square miles of sink-hole marsh. I was then a mile away looking the other way.

A million blackbirds ate duck food only a few yards from where I sat skimming the trackless miles of cattails. Had I known the full story then of this present cloud of redwings, I would probably, out of deference to Glenn's memory, have said something about driving the Ultimate Machine, something about the attitudes of previous owners and present owners. And I might have decided that had I been in the market for a marsh, a dozen square miles of millet now covered with redwings might have been the one thing about this marsh machine that revealed the attitudes of present owners. It would have all come back to this story of the classic vs. the romantic, canals, dams, computer models, decisions to impose human purpose on parts of nature already doing what they did best. It would have all come back to a required sense of what it might take to drive an old planet for a long long time, and what it might take to resist that temptation to put one foot on the gas and the other on the brake, to pop that ultimate machine into reverse while the automatic choke was still on. Small wonder the driving of this marsh produced a result that was not anticipated.

The teal had been nesting, the teal, the coots and grebes, when the decision was made to grasp a wheel valve handle and turn, exactly as the man who did it might have grasped the wheel of his own car and turned, and drain that section of the marsh. They would plant millet, with an airplane, in that drained pond. The millet would mature about the time of fall migration, so they guessed. A dozen square miles of millet would attract ducks and entice them to stay through hunting season; so they guessed. A dozen square miles of millet would attract a redwinged blackbird flock like no human had ever seen, and furthermore, such flock would have stripped those fields of millet before hapless duck ever got its first mouthful; so they never guessed. Nor did they guess that a dozen square miles of marsh drained during teal, coot and grebe nesting season would provide a continuous feast of eggs and chicks for the local skunk and raccoon populations. For days and days, out of the hills and gulleys they came, opportunistic carnivores, searching out now dry nests, coot chicks running frantic over crusted mud where before there had been the comfort of water, water into which a coot chick could disappear in the face of a 'coon. So the furry ones ate themselves fat that year, while the patter of millet seeds from a low-flying aircraft fell above their heads, and no teal were produced by Pond Four that year. The blackbirds loved it.

Thus while I scanned the flats and sloughs, there was also much to occupy my thoughts and visions. I have always been easily distracted, especially by long flying lines of waterfowl and insistent killdeers, grebes slinking into the space between reeds, coots plugging along shore, an occasional heron, watersnake with frog in its mouth, ring-billed gulls and dead fish, crows at hand close for a brief time and the final jamboree before winter tries to close the marsh, seal the top with inches of ice, and turn cattails into brown sticks blowing in the drifts in a Kansas wind. So I crept along slowly, window down, listening to the rotating sky. A fisherman passed, and another, sending clouds of yellow dust across my vision and spattering gravel up on the doors, but still I crept along until I saw a mile away a line of dowitchers asleep. Where there were dowitchers in the fall there would also be yellowlegs, and with this in mind I eased the second-hand Mustang down the dike road, eye always on the flock, until I was as close as I had ever been to a flock of sleeping dowitchers and the few yellowlegs feeding among them.

Thus continued my serious research upon the habits and behavior of the lesser yellowlegs. So intent was I upon the step pattern, the angle of the bill, the starts and stops, and especially my straining to see whether *any* of those feet were topped by an aluminum bracelet, that I never heard the pickup ease up behind on the dike road. I heard the shotgun. It rocked me out of total concentration and pumped the air around my ears. The dowitchers went from full sleep to full flight. And through my binoculars I saw the lesser yellowlegs lying in the mud and behind I heard the pickup door slam and a couple of voices before a young man in jeans jumped long steps down the side of the dike and picked up the bird.

"Sorry about scaring you like that, mister." He was polite and intent, peering down into the Mustang window. "I was so sure one of those birds was banded, but I guess not."

"I'm sure one was banded." The speaker was a much older man, the driver, and he held a spotting telescope in his left hand. "You just shot the wrong bird."

"He's always giving me a raft of garbage about shooting the wrong bird." The younger one spoke directly to me, still stunned behind the wheel. "Drove along one day out here after blackbirds. Must have been a million over in that pond where they planted the millet. Stopped the car and they all flew off, all except one. Shot that one; a female. This guy gives me a raft of garbage over that bird, tells me it's the one bird out of that flock of a million that's sick!"

"Was it?" I asked, beginning to recover.

"You bet! Had its brain full of worms! Never seen *any* thing like that, a brain full of worms! Like to never got all those worms out. Turned out it was just two worms, long and all coiled and twisted around. Old lady redwing had a headache, all right!"

They had all the marks of my profession about them. The younger man now held the bird, preening its feathers back into place, looking carefully beneath the wings, placing the body gently on its back on the fender of his pickup. He started with a small vial of alcohol, and a tiny paintbrush, which he dipped into the vial.

The other end he used to part the feathers. Before it was over he'd looked on and under virtually every feather on the bird's body while the older man chain smoked and once in a while skimmed the marsh with his telescope. The younger man finally plucked a primary flight feather and washed it in the vial, scraping the vane backwards to release a small cloud of mites into the alcohol. I leaned against a back fender and chose the exact time, the exact place, the exact context, the exact countenance, the precise opportunity, to hit him with argot:

"Ever find them down on the tertials?"

"No," he said, stopping for a moment, brush poised. His eyes flickered toward the grin starting to make its way down from the corner of the older man's mouth, then over and through the Mustang window, then up and down me, assessing, evaluating, stopping only for a fraction of a second on the binoculars, before he acknowledged the message behind the question. "No," he said again, "I've never found them on the tertials." He thought for a moment, then sealed the understanding that had never been spoken: "But once in a while on the outer secondaries." And as with the old man Pops, *this* lad also then told a tale of wonder, a tale of death but a tale of life, a tale of values not necessarily misplaced, but differently placed, of curiosity and seeking, of a kind of self-reliance but loneliness of the search, but ultimately, to satisfy that curiosity, of the murder of things he had come to love.

"Read all the bird books you can find, most of them refer to the lesser as simply a smaller version of the greater yellowlegs," he began. "Don't you believe it. They are different birds. Sometimes wonder, I really do, about the psyche of a bird that is always referred to as a smaller version of something else! Figure if that bird ever read all that literature, it would feel ignored, left out, personality suppressed, everything that goes with not having your own life in the eyes of others. Makes a guy wonder whether, if the bird knew all that humans had written about it being only a smaller version of the greater, whether it might feel like some of those women who have no personalities of their own, who have given up their lives entirely to their husbands." He smiled almost as if women who had given up their lives entirely to their husbands were something he had never seen nor known nor studied but had only read about in books. "For one thing, their lice are different. Lice are among the most discriminating animals on the face of the earth. I think sometimes if we all had the discriminatory powers of lice, or some fleas even, how a much better place to live would be this world." He was serious, for a faraway look had come over the younger man's face and he had stopped his work. The body of the bird had been cut open on the hood of the pickup and the man held a yellowlegs heart, cut into, between his fingers. In the other hand, between fingers, he slowly waved dry two glass slides smeared with yellowlegs blood and marked with a diamond pencil on the corner with a special code and records number. The bird's head lay turned and flat against the metal of the hood, bill pointing toward the south. The bird's wings lay loose now, back against the hood. "The lice live down among the feathers and probably eat mostly sloughed off skin and worn protein. Once the bird is dead and the body temperature begins to drop, they leave. It's a death march when a louse leaves a dead host, for there is no way for a louse to march across the sand until it finds another yellowlegs. *Quadraceps falcigerus,*" he said, holding the vial to the light, "the species on the greater is *austini, Quadraceps austini.* Discriminatory as all hell, these lice, but also totally dependent. Make one wonder about whether discriminatory powers invariably lead to total dependence upon something!"

"You're a philosophical son of a bitch," I thought, about the young man who had killed and now was systematically going through, over and around a lesser yellowlegs, all the while considering it a misfortune to have not killed my own banded female!

"I've collected these birds at all seasons they're here, I've collected them in Canada, on the nesting grounds up around Churchill, and I've collected them down on the Gulf Coast in the spring and fall. Going to Argentina next year to collect. May do dowitchers after that. Dowitchers have a tapeworm, you know, a tapeworm that's not like any other tapeworms. Most tapeworms have both sexes in a single animal. This worm, *Shipleya inermis,* has only a single sex, male or female, so it takes two worms to reproduce, not like other tapeworms that can fertilize themselves. Head of that tapeworm gets wadded up into a knot that gets stuck into the wall of the dowitcher intestine, forms a bulge on the outside of the wall. It's a very big worm for a bird that size. Size, sex, pathology, strange way it has of folding that head all up into that little pocket, it's all strange, but none of it as strange as the fact that every dowitcher has one or two of these worms."

It was a beautiful day. He was looking at the horizon almost absentmindedly as he talked, placing the yellowlegs in a plastic bag with a tag on its foot, sealing the bag, and dropping the whole thing into an ice chest that must have been full of dry ice, for it fogged the air when he lifted the lid a crack. In went the bird. Shot-gunned, breast ripped open for a smear of heart blood, feathers meticulously combed for lice and mites, all collected, plastic bagged, sealed, quick frozen, only later to be completely dissected muscle by muscle, bone by bone, drop by drop of thawed intestinal contents, thawed tapeworms, fixed in formalin and alcohol and acetic acid and stained red, studied under a microscope with crusty and ancient exceedingly valuable literature on the table beside, all through the Plains, up on the nesting grounds around Churchill, on the beach in March and on the beach in October, and next year around the edges of an Argentine marsh, went the bird. The potential clash in values loomed as spiral nebulae hurtling toward one another with the speed of light. The legitimate ways of looking at the same machine were as far apart as matter and anti-matter. The legitimate uses, by human, of the same machine, both uses coupled with a feeling of need for understanding of that machine, for understanding the role of that machine in the life of a human, were as different among two scientists as they had been between a scientist and Pops. All followed, or had followed, the yellowlegs, but for the most disparate of reasons. I had not expected to find this pair of men on the marsh that day! The younger continued:

"Ever think about what that really means when *every* bird has one or two worms of a species? Means an ecological relationship with the intermediate host of that worm that is so tight as to be a part of the life of the bird. It means a regulatory mechanism, a mechanism to regulate the population of worms, that functions to override the ultimate effects of such an ecological relationship. Dowitchers get those worms from eating insects, probably, yeah, the larval worm probably lives in insects."

96

I still stared at the place where the yellowlegs had disappeared into the ice chest and thought about the place the yellowlegs, *my* banded yellowlegs, had disappeared into the Kansas sky.

"Every dowitcher, *every dowitcher,* eats enough of that species of insect to get these kinds of worms. Every worm pair exerts a control over its own species' survival so that the dowitcher never gets too infected, overpopulated, you might say. Maybe a pair of worms in a dowitcher gut precludes the establishment of any other pairs. Who knows how this is done? Who in the hell would ever have thought tapeworms were territorial! Relationships between species, dowitchers and worms, tells a great deal about the relationships between other species, dowitchers and beetles, or whatever insect is involved. The transitive laws apply. Beautiful mottled bird is a member of an integral domain." He trailed off into the higher mathematics of dowitchers while the older man smiled and looked from time to time with his telescope out over the marsh. "Wish to hell we'd gotten the banded one. I'm totally sure there was one of those birds that was banded."

"Please don't kill the banded bird."

"Got to, if I can. Been banding those regularly up at Churchill, chicks, need that longevity and seasonal data."

"There is no other way to get the information?"

"Not much, mister, got to mark a bird somehow before you can tell how long it's lived; band's the thing, then got to kill them so you can tell how long they've lived."

"Kill them to tell how long they've lived?"

"Right. You see, the yellowlegs is even more of a mystery than the dowitcher. Long-billed dowitcher nests in a fairly defined geographical area. Yellowlegs nests across broad areas and migrates to places we may never know existed much less were occupied by birds. We know it maintains a dynamic equilibrium relationship with many other species in a variety of environments. It survives in a way we could all emulate . . . "

I was still not sure after my experience with Pops that the yellowlegs had "survived."

"This bird picks up lice as a nestling, its own lice, its own species, and they live on the bird in perfect harmony, never causing the host serious harm, always there in small numbers, maybe even doing the bird a subtle favor by cleaning the skin of detritus that might support a bacterial infection. *Quadraceps falcigerus* is a tradition with yellowlegs, *lesser* yellowlegs, a tradition of dynamic equilibrium association with another species that the bird learns, or acquires—that's a better word, *acquires a tradition*—almost as soon as it's hatched."

I wondered about the possibility of a human baby acquiring a tradition of dynamic equilibrium with other species almost as soon as that human baby was born.

"Bird picks up mites, feather mites, about as soon as it gets flight feathers, and it has to pick those up from the parent. They are tiny, these mites, and they wedge themselves in rows between the barbs of the vanes of the longest flight feathers, out at the tips usually, that's where they ride to Argentina. It would be the same as if you flew to Argentina on a 747 that flapped its wings, and your seat was on the outside of the wingtip. There were times when I was younger," said the young man, "when I thought I was going crazy, when I thought there was no place on earth for me. Then I saw the mites in the barbs in the vanes of the longest yellowlegs flight feathers, and I said to myself, 'There is a place for everything in this world, and there is a way to live in constant turbulence, there is a way to find a place where you can live in peace and harmony with your immediate and larger supportive environment, a place where maybe the multitudes that desire life comforts cannot envision, a place for a feather mite, a place of your own at the end of a yellowlegs wing. After seeing the place the feather mites had chosen, I knew it was up to me to choose my place, not let others do it for me, and to find the good in that place, to extract what I needed from it, my mental needs as well as physical needs, but not destroy that place in the process."

"Must be a gas riding to Argentina stuck in the wingtips of a yellowlegs!"

"Couldn't be anything else!" replied the younger, a wry turn to the corner of his mouth. "Bird picks up worms, too, picks up worms in the Northern Hemisphere and transports them to the Southern Hemisphere, picks up worms in the Southern Hemisphere and transports them into the Northern Hemisphere. *Kowalewskiella totani,* that's the name of the worm it brings in the spring, brings in from Argentina. Worms can't live in this country, though, die before the yellowlegs reach Canada. Beautiful worm, tapeworm, absolutely beautiful. Hooks, suckers; beautiful! Here you got another case of a tight ecological relationship you know the bird participates in off in some corner of the world, but you don't know how or where. Bird is a machine itself, functions in highly coordinated ways we've never analyzed, with integrated parts, feedback informational flow, activations of programs in the brain. But it's also a part of a larger machine, and it functions as a part of that larger machine, that Ultimate Machine. You can see it as an integral part of the Ultimate Machine in those relationships with those creatures that depend on it, the tapeworms, lice, feather mites."

"Ultimate Machine?"

"Earth. You're also a part of it, mister."

"I guess I had already about decided that."

"You some kind of bird club or something? Not too many people go around with Leitz binoculars."

"I guess you could say I was some kind of bird club."

The younger man introduced himself and his older friend. "This is Homer, last of the old-time naturalists." I shook hands with Homer. Our fingers were still in contact when the man's face turned back toward the marsh and a long cigaret ash fell off into the gravel road to be blown away another time.

"What do you hope eventually to gain, to learn, to accomplish in all this research?" From back in my temporary permit powdered old white Mustang came the Statler Brothers out of a local station.

"Everywhere a person turns there are reputations, national reputations, international reputations, to be made in science. Just have to pick the right thing. My research on the parasite fauna of the yellowlegs has already netted me three publications, several papers given at national meetings, my name is becoming known and associated with shorebird biology, with parasite population dynamics. I should get my doctorate easily within a year, already have a good post-doc lined up in Alaska, another possibility in Europe, another down in Georgia." The Last of the Old Time

Naturalists touched him on the arm and pointed out over the marsh. The younger man talked while his own binoculars went to his eyes and aimed in the direction of the finger.

"Person has to be good nowdays to land a job at a good university. Has to have publications, has to have already proven himself as a scientist. Takes a great deal to be competitive. I will be competitive; I will be competitive as all living hell. I will milk this yellowlegs system for all it's worth and when I'm through, I'll be an ecologist, an ecologist on a global scale, with a reputation and a publication list, graduate students with publication lists, grant money." The young man dreamed out on the dike, still staring with his binoculars at the cattail line. "Who knows, I may end up a university president some day!" He turned back with another wry grin. "Hire Homer here as my vice-chancellor!"

"Play hell hirin' me as any vice-chancellor!" said Homer, and I wondered if Homer were interested in following the yellowlegs in an old Ford car.

"Yellowlegs system is one of a lifetime of systems a guy can study. Just happens to be a good one, mainly because of the very specific lice, mites, and a series of tapeworms. The bird is an n-dimensional hyperspace for a community of other animals, a pulsating hyperspace, pulsating with its physiological state during breeding season. During migration, on an annual basis, the hyperspace pulsates and changes and the animal community *you* call yellowlegs must also pulsate. The fact that *Kowalewskiella totani* is lost as the birds return is an observation of one period of pulsation. Each part of the yellowlegs is a resource base; sometimes that base expands, sometimes it contracts, but each time it changes the animal community changes with it, all in a dynamic equilibrium. Learn how the yellowlegs system operates and you may discover the key to an intelligent use of this n-dimensional hyperspace known as Earth. Hell, there might even be a Nobel Prize waiting for me down at the end of the yellowlegs trail!"

"Got a flock, small flock, off north of that dike down on Pond Three," said Homer.

The younger man turned his binoculars to that mud slough to the north of the dike down on Pond Three. The wind was still and the sounds of ducks carried over the marsh from who knew how far away. The Statler Brothers were still on the Mustang radio, some song about someone having already been down some road, been somewhere, having more years on some life, being patient because of it, some song like that. I looked at the younger scientist and might as well have been staring into the mirror of time. The number of "systems" such as yellowlegs a person could "milk" was beyond the imagination of any single human. I had milked a few systems myself a few times, always coming away with a pail of something. The "something" had always been tangible; data, hard data, numbers on entry lines in data books, data sets in computers, formulae, numbers, typing on a page of high quality bond paper, photographs, graphics well designed, grant applications, money, accounts. I had always concluded I was in the right business, that my "career" was progressing along normal lines and would someday lead to the places of appropriate challenge, appropriate recognition, appropriate responsibility and public visibility for one of my talents. Recognition, responsibility and visibility were always assumed to constitute achievement, for along with them came a new measure of awe. Challenge was something different. The challenge sometimes accompanied recognition and visibility, but one could seek the latter without seeking the former. Staring at the young man through time and seeing only myself as a child, I tried to find where I had gone astray, why it was my own trail had led finally to the dikes looking at yellowlegs, while the young man's had started on the dikes looking at yellowlegs. I was swept away by a cycle, of sequence-programmed events not unlike a cell cycle, and I began dissecting my life as maybe would the world's grubbiest ornithologist dissect the life of a bird to discover the events that triggered departures.

There had been a time back not long before I was the age of this aggressive young biologist, when cell division was a thing called "mitosis," and mitosis was pictured in books as chromosome movements. But division of the cell was no longer "mitosis," instead it was the "cell cycle," of which mitosis was only an insignificant but ultimately necessary part. The significant part, the control events, occurred at other times, times we used to think the cell was resting. The synthesis of genetic information occupied much of the cell's time long before mitosis ever occurred. Prior to that synthesis and following that synthesis, cells often retreated into private times in which they "prepared" for subsequent events, and no one knew whether that preparation was active or passive. It might well be only a cell decision to be vulnerable to certain influences; thus passive. It might be a precisely executed set of reactions irrevocably committing the cell to future precisely executed sets of reactions; thus active. Only a select few cell types could ever go back into "the cycle," i.e., reproduce again. Those that could never go back were differentiated. Standing on the dike road, I knew I was differentiated, I *had* differentiated, and could never return to the cycle of learning new lives. But then I thought back over my years as a teacher and concluded that in teaching, *true* teaching, a human stayed forever in the cycle, forever *mentally* reproductive, *intellectually* reproductive. I knew that humans were so capable of differentiations into professions, higher orders of differentiations, some of which shut off their powers of intellectual reproduction. I wondered even then if a choice to become a teacher could be the differentiation into a state of continual intellectual reproduction; I wondered even then what *kind* of teacher one would have to be to remain in the cycle as a role; and I concluded that a person who could pass along a lasting vision of the world would be such a teacher. There has been one of those in my past; he worked on cars like the one I bought from Pops. In the end they called him "Master Mechanic." He provided me with a vision of what this young scientist had just called the "Ultimate Machine."

And I have called the yellowlegs a machine and in doing so have established the difference between yellowlegs and humans. While all parts of a yellowlegs' body are produced by differentiations, the bird is nevertheless incapable of the higher order of differentiations which are routinely accomplished by humans. Those differentiations produce politicians, lawyers, professors, doctors, bums and ornithologists from the cell cycles of youth. Similarly, no machine set is capable of those higher orders of differentiation that humans accomplish. Machine sets and things like yellowlegs are thus somewhat equivalent in this regard; they evolve, they spread into different roles as an evolutionary process, not an ontogenetic one, and especially not, as in humans, purposeful ontogenetic processes. There was obviously some sense within a Master Mechanic that recognized such essential differences between men and machines, and then refused to let machines take over all human functions, values and decisions. Such a Master Mechanic's sense resisted, too, the takeover inclinations of those purely mathematical machines— no, not computers, but mathematical equivalents of machines: organizations, administrations, rule sets, obligation sets that produced reactions allowable only within certain tolerances, often tolerances within thousandths of inches. Retain the strictly human options, the *best* of what the word *human* implied, i.e., the creative options—that was the true message from a Master Mechanic to Man: don't let machine control person. But in order to prevent machine from controlling person to the point of destroying person, person had to place machine in its proper role, had to understand its limitations as well as its advantages, and had to understand that in the long run the former might outweigh the latter!

"You know, a guy could just take chicken wire and probably build a walk-in trap. Set it out along one of those sloughs with some leads. Catch all sorts of stuff, of course, but nevertheless, wouldn't have to actually kill the birds if you caught your yellowlegs. Seen one before," I said almost absentmindedly, calling into play now one of my best acts for a peer, or superior, or a gullible administrator: the musing dummy. A standard teaching technique—the musing dummy—an act proper and useful for a useful and proper place and time. "Seen one before. Had a different sort of place than this, but it probably should still work. Curve the walls around so they make a funnel opening here, string your leads out along the banks like this for a hundred yards or so." I drew the plans in the dirt with my boot toe.

"Never work," said the young man. "Besides, still have to kill the birds to get the worms out, to do the thing properly."

"Work like a charm," said Homer, smiling, great gaps closed at places where a filter Salem was held between his teeth, ashes blowing back into his eyes, squinting, leather folds with two days' growth of gray stubble, stiff as wire, "work like a charm! Catch them sumbitches up at the ends of all these sloughs! Place out by upper end of Pond Three, catch a trainload!"

"Think about it a little bit," said the musing dummy, "all kinds of information a guy could get out of a walk-in trap." I raised my

103

binoculars and looked at exactly the place Homer was staring with his telescope. The young man stood looking but with binoculars still swinging at his waist. "Put that bird in a plastic bag with its head sticking out, shoot in a shot of insecticide, then comb out all those lice and mites without having to go through each feather like that." Homer was nodding, telescope still affixed to the horizon. "Take a blood smear, run serology on a sample, tell if the animal is carrying some virus, wash out the cloaca for tapeworm eggs, take your worm samples you already got and computer analyze their eggs, then set up a counter, a particle counter like they got at every hospital to count blood cells, run those eggs through it, gives you a profile analysis of the particles in bird shit, identify your worms that way, take worm samples from birds you already got frozen, grind 'em up and inject a chicken, make some antibodies to worm, then add a worm check to your serology; it's all that easy. With antibodies we're talking species-specific proteins, you know that, can't get a better identification tool than that. Do all this stuff without killing the bird, that allows you to measure all your parameters on the same animal over and over again. In theory you could follow a single bird all the way from Canada to Argentina and back again, measuring those parameters all along the way. That'd be a study make your eyes pop out!" I glanced sideways at the younger scientist and forced a poker face. "Simple technological advance like a chicken wire walk-in trap allows you to study the *dynamics* of your animal, *rates* at which they acquire lice, mites, after you've cleaned them, weights of birds themselves as they migrate, amount of energy actually budgeted for egg production, raising young, protection against predators, all that."

"Follow a single bird! Follow a single yellowlegs from Canada to Argentina and back again! My God what a study that would be!"

"Might have to take some time off," I said.

"Work like a charm, just like a damn charm!" said Homer. "Set that sumbitch up right out there upper end of Three. Goin' in to town now, pick up the wire, drink a couple beers." He turned to the younger man, still staring at a senior scientist who in turn kept his eyes glued through binoculars at a non-place on the horizon. "Goin'?" The young man still stared, thinking; the whirlings of his mind almost stirred the dust on a gravel dike road. "Goin'?"

"Take all that data you've been generating, fit it into a computer to analyze the actual resource sets used by the various members of that community you call a yellowlegs, then add the *dynamics* of that community, the numbers that actually tell of the pulsations and equilibrium gives and takes, with a walk-in trap and analysis of live birds."

Homer revved the pickup a time or two, still absently scanning the marsh.

"Computer's great. Our finest machine. Chicken-wire trap gives you the best stuff to go into your computer, into your finest machine. Simple consideration, thinking yourself of a chicken-wire trap, lets the highest machine be applied without killing the community."

Homer called out from back in the cab. "Goin' in to town, chancellor! Get that friggin' chicken wire, drink a couple beers, catch them sumbitches up in Three!"

"Every idiot's got a computer doing his thing nowdays. Not too many folks got walk-in traps nor places to put them. Chicken wire will get you out in front in your game and keep you there for a few years."

"A single yellowlegs, alive all the way from Canada to Argentina! God what a study!"

Homer leaned on the horn; a half-dozen coots pattered across the marsh in response.

"Have a good trip; wherever it is you're going." The young man was stepping high into the pickup; Homer was still grinning.

"I will," I said to the road dust and truck bed and the image of a young scientist heading toward town, seen through the back window talking, gesturing to Homer, outlining with his hands what could only have been the latest modification of a walk-in trap before the first model had ever been built. These meetings between scientists always produce combinations of ideas, new applications. The marshes always provide an escape, serene and idyllic times, for scientists to meet and discuss their things. A meeting of scientists in a marsh would always produce a good feeling, the calm of synthesis before the storm of application, the satisfaction of thoughts and ideas that were themselves the products of science, not the machine or data or graphics, but the relief that the major

105

work, thinking, had been done and now only the technicons need go finish the job.

I have often felt such euphoria after scientific meetings. Perhaps everyone does, and thus perhaps this is why scientists have meetings. They come together, talk of ambitions and dreams that everyone understands, of experiments and studies in a tongue familiar to all, of data, of animals, of relationships, of high and wondrous things that no common person knew, much less thought about, much less studied. The ritual of the termite people— touching thoughts, some even taking the rejected ideas of others, thus passing a thread of experience, all of it reaffirming the faith in exploration—was my communion on the marsh with my younger self. The younger self had never even said, "Thank you," and I cared not. An old idea was everyone's property, and a combination of old and young idea was everyone's responsibility. I suppose there might have been some pitiful souls back in the dark reaches of a laboratory who would have considered a walk-in trap linked to a computer as a private technological advance for which one should receive proper credit. But these were not the ones who would ever be dragged out into the sunlight with all their mental roaches, taken to the river, and baptized into the discipline of the romantic.

The total satisfaction of a day of accomplishment swept over me as I sat behind the wheel of the used machine. How fortunate to be in this profession! The teacher, the tricks the teacher employs to move the thought processes of those younger and smarter than a musing dummy: what could be a better profession for a human! What monumental luck it was to be out in the middle of a marsh having just synthesized a combination of chicken wire and silicon chips! What other human could even hope for such a life, such a heady life, except the biology teacher! Why, I had things no other human had: a marsh, the temporary company of a young and ambitious scientist, the acquaintance of Homer, a used Ford Mustang, and a bird to follow. I would migrate ahead of the bird this time; the confidence of success out on the dike road throbbed within me, sharpened to a razor edge my senses and nerves! I would go south and wait; let the bird come to me! I knew the place from my own youth, as surely as the bird now getting restless at the upper end of Pond Three knew that place: an island in a sea of black machinery all pumping for black liquid, all three hundred miles over the prairie to the south.

I considered stopping in the nearest town to shout my scientific accomplishment from a convenient street corner. But in the back of my mind was an image of myself in muddy jeans and worn field jacket, not-yet-licensed well-used car parked alongside, a forty-year-old vagrant, shouting down on Mainstreet, U.S.A., that I had just told another how to combine chicken wire with a computer to catch a gray bird on its way to Argentina so the tapeworm eggs could be sized and counted and the lice could be saved, all with Government money and all without killing the bird! Instead, I drove eighty miles an hour for a while on a dirt road as straight and endless as a theoretical figure in geometry. Soon I would cross over into the other world, a world *I* call "The Tropics," and soon there would be a sign with a friendly cowboy and a friendly Indian proclaiming this other world had been reached.

Somewhere in the night the dirt became red. When I stopped for gas, the people talked in another way, and I knew I had passed the sign.

10 ⌒ In the Tropics

*. . . anyone wanting to contact
him hereafter had best try Outer
Mongolia or Oklahoma.*

Irons S. Pendleton

*T*hey say that in the tropics the environmental complexity
is great compared to the north and that in the tropics there are
many sorts of places that are not present in the temperate zones.
There are physical places in the tropics and species that don't live
elsewhere and lush vegetation that grows from the depths of sea
level to the spiral heights of cloud forests. They also say that a
person can draw graphs of the world, graphs that show the number
of swallowtail butterfly species per area the size of Potawattomi
County, and that such numbers go up and up until one reaches the
Equator then go down and down again until one stands on the harsh
dirt of Tierra del Fuego. These same persons say the same principle
applies wherever one travels, this principle that says when an
environment is complex, it supports a greater diversity of types
than do less complex environments. The diversity of types occupy
each and every one their own places in nature, their niches, and for
one who conjures up an elongate space in catacomb wall at use of
the word "niche," some surprises are in store. "Niches," places to
live, nowadays are complicated mathematical places, abstract
places, although one must wonder if it all matters to a hummingbird species stuck away forever in a single valley, whiling away

the days competing with large bees for binding sites on dripping obscene flowers.

The complexity of life, itself a mystery, is thus manifest in complexities upon complexities as one migrates, unerring but south, toward an Equator, and these multiple complexities compound themselves until relationships are established, then higher orders of relationships established, then analysis valid for relationships becomes valid for relationships between relationships, until before long the hummingbird is projected through outerspace transformational machinery into an abstract n-dimensional hypervolume, "n" taking values between zero and infinity but losing all tangible sense at values greater than four!

In the night my steed entered "The Tropics," and the tropical culture engulfed us at the gas stop. So did the dirt; the red dirt. Off in the half-night just beyond filling station lights I could see the packed red clay as I could see the red stains ground into tires, fender wells, and door paint of the station pickup, parked for the evening in the station bay, waiting for a break in the action so the young attendant could git time t' give 'er a oyal chainge. The banded yellowlegs flew over, high in the dark, and had I heard the plaintive call from up in the void, I would not have responded. I knew where we were both going. But she would dally along the way, and I would lowgrowl it on down the open highway for four hours until I got there. We were both in familiar territory now, and the swirl of activities that characterized this young land was a comforting swirl. The multitude of options available to a free-seeking person in a complex society cleared my mind the way Kansas, for all my love of that state, could never do.

Four corners of America meet here in the tropics I call "Oklahoma," but not quite with closure, for down the middle still lies a strip of plains. Furthermore, that strip is itself marked in half by an imaginary line I now straddled in my used automobile. To the east of the imaginary line lay an ocean of tall grass prairie; to the west lay a mirror image ocean of short grass prairie. From the northwest there ran a ridge of montain uplands that finished not too far inside the line, pulling, enticing, haunting, often against their will, montain species southward and eastward until they just made it into the Land of the Red Man. There in that place those species encountered a Panhandle. Mountain bluebird and magpie traveled the hospitable land until they ran smack into the sage and dunes and wheat as far as the human eye could see, and there they stopped short. The northeast forest culture also dipped into the tropics, with blackjack oaks that made crooked faints posts for rusted barbed *wyar* and hills that made twisting giant lakes out of pork barrel dams and Indian tribal land.

From the southeast the oak-pine forests, spreading in antebellum laziness across the land from frenetic Atlanta, stretched and softly but with the confidence of possession laid an impoverished hand on *the family's corner* and in doing so made a place for a red-cockaded woodpecker and a pine-pitch spattered hole. Not to be outdone, from the southwest the Edwards Plateau sent some representative types, uplands, granite mountains, crystal lake with pink boulders, and a firing range where generations of startlingly young men had directed the withering practice fire of mammoth weapons against an Indian landmark called Signal Mountain. Mostly to no avail; the mountain still stood.

This congress of geography produced a lengthy list of life forms for this tropical place, human as well as animal and plant, behavioral as well as structural, in business and in pleasure. If there is one thing I have learned from time spent in these tropics, it is that such environmental complexity often destroys most of what could be called intellectual conservatism; or reserved unwillingness to gamble, or be different; or worry about doing too well. What an attitude! And it could not have been better symbolized than by this tropical nation's army, and it could not have been manifest more strongly than in the seasonal wars. When the wars came, this tropical culture fielded a smart-talking army with a rebellious coal-black leader, sallied forth across the boundaries, and laid to waste the best efforts of dozens of grown men working with numbered paladins on a plastic carpet with lines.

Now first there was the matter of oyal, or oll, or awl, as in "them awl wells out in th' wess pastchure," with accent on the *past,* where in the real past there had slogged dying bands of cultures now forgotten except in the State Historical Society Museum. And out in the wess pastchure Angus cattle wore very narrow trails through the bloody clay beneath those derricks out across the overgrazed fields to a waterin' tank, itself filled with what might have been tomato soup. Some men in the world's greasiest clothes populated such well sites, "well sites" being a pretty easily understood term that was almost never used in the parlance of business.

No, the "well site" was really the "Johnson No. 1," or "Johnson No. 3," "Johnson No. 2" having been a very expensive dry hole, all located on what had been the original Johnson land leased for years by Tidewater, who never drilled two feet, but who had finally bought outright one fourth of the mineral rights from the Johnson heirs, Wilma Johnson, unmarried sister of Betty Lou Johnson, early wife of Henry Swantek, daughter also of the original Johnson people, and aunt of the Swantek kids, two of whom had moved to California where they'd gone into the real estate business, except that Genevieve Swantek had subsequently gotten a divorce and married a tavern owner back in Bakersfield, where she'd worked part-time behind the bar. But her first husband had died, and his people didn't remember her new man's name, and probably didn't remember it because they never did like her very well and they liked him even less. But Wilma, who was still alive down in the white house behind all those forsythia and spirea hedges, was going blind and couldn't remember where her last letter was but thought maybe one of Genevieve's kids was still in the Army, so maybe the young man trying to get the lease documents in order could try the Army, maybe *they* could trace down the locations of all who needed to sign in front of a notary before the bulky rock-hard man with a finger missing and the world's greasiest clothes could move his rig in, order up some used drill pipe to be delivered to the Johnson No. 4 out in the wess pastchure and drop it in a rack so a donkey could snake it up the rig, and the diesel engine in total command could force it down into the ground toward the Wilson Shale which would then provide the crude to pay for all this.

The young man with the lease documents did just fine until one day on the hot streets of Bakersfield, he discovered that Genevieve had a child by her first husband, actually one of several children by her first husband, but that *this* child was institutionalized and *his* portion of the lease signature had to deal with the whole matter of legal and protective state guardians, not to mention the fact that

Genevieve's youngest daughter was the ambitious one and thought the family ought to get five dollars an acre more for the lease than Sunoco was offering for the three-fourths minerals Tidewater had not purchased and which would now *neverever* be sold outright as long as there's a producin' wail in th' *countyanywhere*. In the meantime a middle-aged geologist sat in a lonely office over maps with microcircles and contour lines showing the lay of formations a thousand feet below the Johnson pastchure and decided again that there *was* awl in that dome and tapped his worn shoes with a scientist's impatience over the leasing troubles. And while he tapped, Wilma died, and her estate, what there was of it, was turned over to "the lawyers." The geologist had learned long ago that there *were* lawyers, usually in firms with two members, in almost every one of these little towns like Wilma lived in. The young company man had some surprises in store when he returned from California.

As if Wilma's death were not enough, there was the matter of surface damages at No. 2, and although Genevieve's youngest daughter had not visited the family property, she was convinced they'd have to sue for the full amount, 'cause them drillers'd made a bigger mud pit or took out more of a faints or something, she'd not fully understood the day those equipments rolled in across agricultural land. The fact that there were crops on that land meant nothing to any of them. Agricultural land would never be the sacred garden it might be in other places, it was only that surface damages were *always* part of the deal. So with violation of a maize field reduced to a dollar quibble over surface damages, a quibble that would have occured even if the Johnson No. 2 had been drilled in the local dump, I, the old tropical traveler who knew all this well, began to see the ecological diversity, the lack of specialization, that in turn spawned the richness of this rebellious place into which a yellowlegs flew and into which I piloted a white craft with black stripe through the night.

Immersed in this atmosphere of complexity and machinery, my thoughts returned to the Master Mechanic who had lived among all this, who had through his life and death passed along that romantic world view necessary for a human's proper relationship with things technical, things sophisticated, things of monumental complexity that must be felt, not understood. Had I known how soon I was to be tested by machinery requiring the touch of the Master Mechanic, I would still have never stopped, have never eased that machine carrying me through the Oklahoma night. I *had* his insights, he'd given them to me as a death present; I was always confident alone on the highway, and I am still always confident alone on the highway. I have no fears of machinery, of things technical, for I have my world view. I can fix a Ford almost any day, any night. Had I known how soon that confidence was to be tested, I would never have stopped. Rockport, though, Rockport is a different story. I still don't know now, if I had known of the impasse that awaited me in Rockport then, if I would have handled it differently. And oh God was I headed for impasse in Rockport. And did I ever put things technical into some kind of perspective in Rockport. And I am glad today that I once knew a Master Mechanic.

The lights of a rig off west of the interstate flickered through blowing trees along a darkened creek. Weeds blew across through the traffic, and a very dirty semi loaded with strange giant machinery blinked its lights then came around with a vengeance, disappearing down the long hill through a front door opened by a trucker many miles further on this same highway. My heart quickened, for the excitement of this land always quickens the heart, the excitement of *knowing* there is much to think about in this tropical place, that there are many places to live, many thoughts to think with plenty of company so no one thinks strange thoughts are strange. Yes, it was good to be in Oklahoma! I smiled; stretched back against the seat and thought of a life as one who studied wild things, whose role in the world was to teach the world of these wild things, whose responsibility it was perhaps even to evangelize that love for a single aging banded lady gray bullet bird on her way for the last time to Argentina.

Such pleasant thoughts engulfed and lulled and erased all worries and concerns and put my mind totally at ease. You might have figured it, right? When the alternator bearings exploded and froze it took a few minutes to get my mind back down out of those clouds. Quick order: rapid fire whir engine speed mechanical whir whining to higher pitch smell of something burning temperature rising frayed and finally burned fan belt clattering for a time under the hood before falling out to become a rubber snake for tomorrow's child watching the miles pass from the back of a station wagon. It would be light by the time the family passed the stalled Mustang. The child would watch the man and the Mustang recede and he would wonder what people did with car trouble so far from town. I waved. The kid waved back. That was one of eleven million cars that passed before I started into town. You don't want to know the name of that town. Don't ever have car trouble down in Oklahoma. Glenn's dead. He didn't live in that town anyway. Let me tell you what it's like having trouble in Oklahoma, trouble with your machines. I'm going to relate all this stuff very carefully. Remember this is a scientist, not some rinky-dink, but a scientist, doing *research,* not fiddling with his shoelaces, but *research.* Like I said, when you're out on the highway next time doing research, don't never have no car trouble down in the tropics!

I started off walking in the heating blowing fall morning and looked for seven miles across a dry green pastchure slightly rolling gullies, raked gashes through what seemed a granular thin layer of dirt, not soil, but dirt, red, granular, *dirt,* toward a grain elevator's buff cylinders signaling a town where there might live and work a man who understood machines: machines that combined the Johnson wheat, giant specter reaper beetles attended even through the night by trucks with red staked slats and fine white scrollwork; machines that coughed and exploded their days away in black/ brown environments rotating the floor of a drilling rig; machines built outa De-troit to power a self-contained mobile home in turn containing a petroleum laboratory of untold complexity, now sittin' back in the Chrysler agency up on jackstands while the young Halliburton man sat down at the hotel coffee shop off in the corner of the lunch counter; machines that pumped pink mud, *special* mud; machines that cracked crude and dealt out products to make gasoline, plastic, drugs and stereo records; machines that simply plowed fields; machines that hauled black cattle with red-stained legs; machines that carried older boys to a rodeo with all the in-crowd dress, walk, talk, injury, pickup truck/horse trailer/bale of hay and girl with teased hair and teased cowboy; and, I hoped, stomping on the gravel towards that town, my mind sorting through all the places for a yellowlegs to land, an older model Ford alternator.

I slipped into those same dreams that come every time with rote walking, and I flew then on gray wings toward a place called Argentina, along the way sorting through a place with so many places to be, to stop, to live, so many ways to while away the months, so many niches, that ecological diversity into which anyone or anything could slip unnoticed and find solace. It was there before I understood: silent gold chrome power machine, an eagle on the hood, twin CB antennae, and a spatter of apron gravel thrown by airplane quality radials. I touched the door gingerly, not seeing through one-way mirrors that made all the windows of such a special Cadillac. The door opened and behind the wheel there lay coiled a man with molded steel black black cable arms and blacker sunglasses, leather wide-brimmed hat and a string of beads that could only have been purest African.

"Got some car trouble. Need a ride up to the next town."

The man nodded, raised his chin slightly and when I looked again, we were at highway speeds.

"I'm a scientist; I study birds, one species in particular right now, right now until I had that car trouble. Alternator, I think, sounded like an alternator." My voice seemed too loud.

Silence.

"I said I'm a scientist; studying birds. Some amazing things to learn about birds, about life. Swainson's hawk over there, up on the pole. Southern prairie's a great place for hawks in the fall. Even a better place in the spring. Drive down this highway in the spring you can see 'em catching things, mice, cotton rats, right along this road. Fall's okay; not as good as spring. Redtail flying over on your side; probably an immature."

Silence.

"Got a roughleg over on your side now. Highly variable in color, roughlegs. That one's got more dark in it than you'd expect." It was out before I knew it was out; but then it was only the biological truth! "Polymorphic; that's the word for a species that has many color phases."

Still silence. There was a flicker of white behind black glasses. A dark hand drifted to the dials and the CB rushed into life. The man spoke a language I had never heard. The words were English. The grammar was something else.

"Good instrument, the CB. Good idea to be able to communicate, especially out on the highway, say a person has some car trouble, just call up some help. Animals communicate, too, make some sounds, assume postures within a certain context. Posture and context, that's what adds meaning to an animal's sounds, just posture and context. Sometimes that's all there is, only posture and context. In humans we call it 'paralanguage'; paralanguage can say more than the spoken word. Now you take this bird I'm working on. Has a lot of different calls, depending on the situation and on what it wants to communicate. Some behavior, too, makes all the difference in the world when the bird makes that behavior along with the calls." The exit ramp appeared and moved toward us in a gentle arc. The panther spoke a lowgrowl communication.

"You bein' *paid* f' this, man?"

"No, I guess I'm not. I guess when you get right down to it, I'm the one who's doing the paying." My foot was on the ground and the wind blew and the colors were different, half into the natural environment, the real world, the earthy smell rural red state cattle oyal maize real world. Back buried in the power machine a pearl smile crept over the panther.

"Catchin' the roughlegs on *mye* side; fine a black one!"

I stood for a moment in the wind, wondering what I was doing, then remembered. Teaching has a way of consuming your thoughts, transporting you to another world somewhere, especially minority education. I have never felt I ever did anything for a black student. There is a tragedy there somewhere. I hope the guy sees a black roughlegs every day for the rest of his life. I tramped on toward a crumble of buildings. Like I said before in that fit of charity: don't never have no car trouble down in the tropics 'less you just *have* to.

"Need an alternator; '67 Ford 289."

The man's lips moved apart but it was not a smile, more an involuntary movement baring fangs, an inheritance from some primeval pre-human that for some stupid reason surfaced in this generation in this place. The primate was sallow and sunken, and moved among gray boxes and gray metals, reaching as they all do to very large books subdivided, braced in a holder, and flipped pages, flipped, flipped, flipped, flipped back, then in another book beside the first, flip, flip flip flip flip flip flip back, run finger up and down column of figures; "no"; flip back, turn to another book, flip flip, hesitate, flipflipflipflip, "here we go; no, that's for the full size; air conditioned? No, okay, here we go." My vision blurred and those flipping pages became yellowlegs' wings, a book of yellowlegs' wings, a whole world, an entire world of machinery and spare parts catalogued in books of yellowlegs' wings. He disappeared back into shelves, returned as might some cat with a dead wren, turned the box, added tax on a machine with a mechanical lever, told price, sank back into position while his lips again parted in a non-smile over teeth. Phone makes short ring and some part discussed with eye on girlie calendar three years old. Phone still wedged between chin and shoulder, cash ticket taped to alternator box, rebuilt alternator, primate turns back to divided books, pages flip flip . . . off in shop back around corner large engine explodes into life, idles roughly then is shut off with stream of language, radio talks about local schedule tonight and tomorrow at Lewis Field pot-bellied man in double knit orange pants white shirt black tie white shoes off-colored glasses and shirt pocket with plastic liner with pencils calls out from showroom with one new car, call echos, echos—

"Sail yew a newe one!"

"No, thanks anyway." I mumbled something about a bird beneath my breath. I was a half-mile down the road before remembering the fan belt was also broken. Kid with grease gun at first filling station pokes head out from under old Chevy up on rack and wipes nose at a migrating ecologist.

"Don' carry no fanbelts. Chick own at haff mal more, Skilly stashun."

Flip flip flip more pages through Skelly manual of parts, driveway bell clanging, help interrupted, finding number myself, owner returning, finding number again, phone ringing, flips through book with phone wedged under chin, driveway bell clanging, blond with weaverbird nest of hair flutters bills, owner returns, finds a belt, driveway bell clanging, clanging . . .

Like I said, don't never have no car trouble in the tropics 'less there's no other place to have it. Had to flag down a kid in a pickup for tools. Threw the old alternator in the trunk. The thing actually started. Something about scientific research that not a lot of people realize: there's all this machinery you have to deal with, spectrophotometers, pH meters, centrifuges, ultra-centrifuges, electron microscopes, pipet washers, gas chromatographs, fraction collectors, autoclaves, incubators, binoculars, Ford cars. Like to have seen old Glenn with an electron microscope.

Out on the interstate crows battled the wind out of an orange sky, peeling off from a dead rabbit as carloads of high school kids passed on their way to Friday night games at neighboring towns, into the streaking sky now with great slashes of red orange and blue gray and con trails out of Wichita. Cars had headlights on now, buffeted by wind, wind pumping windows, through darkening rows of tossing trees, the whine of tires, a flashing red and blue strobe from across the interstate, tail lights as far across the plains as you can see, smell of hit skunk, cars with Texas tags appearing out of the void and disappearing into the void all that quickly, many horse trailers, semi after semi with drill pipe and casing, campers and large boats, headlights oncoming across the Cimarron as far as the horizon, and once the hint of an owl flaring at the traffic. It was very dark now and the scores were coming in, and my head and stomach hurt and I was starving but I also knew from having spent years in this place that the signs said fall was going to end. The bird would be gone, perhaps gone forever, considering what there was to face on a lonely flight to Argentina, so although my head nodded, and I rolled down the window to keep awake, I never considered stopping in Oklahoma until I came to that one place where I knew that a migrating yellowlegs ignoring all the tumultuous goodtime existence below it, would stop. Then a heater hose blew and steam slammed back against the windshield and left billows trailing and the temperature started up and up. I remember at this point being very tired.

Even in the approaching fall, the tropics were warm; even in the steady night wind, the land hung on to fading summer as if it belonged to this nation; even the elm trees, bent from youth by a southern breeze, still had their leaves. I could hear them tossing as again I walked the flint apron through darkness toward lights. I was tired, exhausted, frustrated with troubles from a machine, encoun-

118

tered while chasing a machine, which in turn responded to the changing seasons of the Ultimate Machine, none of it truly understood or appreciated by robots. Times like these, little things have a way of taking over your mind. Cunning, that's the right word, I remember being oh so *cunning* that night. Buy the hose clamps right along with the heater hose this time! The feel for a broken machine, a feel taught by example by an ancient Master Mechanic, applied by a biologist to the Ultimate Machine, that feel was always there! Buy hose clamps! How many of you would have thought to buy the clamps, too? Not many. Besides, I've had car trouble in the Tropics. Learned a few things from that. Most of what I learned is not to do it if you don't have to.

"Way-ell, give y'all three courters; have t' git fi-ive ates own in t'ward town."

"How far in toward town?"

"Haff mal; haff mal on rat. Phillips stashun." Somewhere out in the bay an end wrench fell and bounced; end wrenches have a special sound bouncing on concrete. "Ain't that rat, Lonnie, git fi-ive ates heater hose in at Phillips?" Somewhere from back in the garage Lonnie appeared.

"Got yerse'f some heater hose troubles?"

"Need some five eights."

"Got a piece in here took off ole boy's car issmornin'; *give* it to y' if y'all wants it." Lonnie fished around in a bulk oil can then fished around in another before coming up with a piece of five-eights hose. "Alriddy throwed it away," said Lonnie, "you out on the innerstayte?"

"I'm parked out on the innerstayte."

"Need some clamps?"

"I do need a couple of clamps."

"They'll cost y'allittle. Hose here got a split down own this inn, cut *that* off, use the ress. You'll be okay for a ways yet."

I paid for the clamps.

"Care for a little dope?"

"Pardon me?"

"Care for a little dope? Lonnie an' me's smokin' a little dope; grows rat at back here; want some?"

"No, thanks."

"Beer? Got Coors."

"No, thanks." But three hundred yards back toward the highway I changed my mind.

"Six-pack Bud."

"Chainged yer mind, huh?" The kid's face had a grin that said "atta boy, drink a little beer!" and he swept the six-pack out of a glass-front refrigerator up on the counter and rung up the sale all with a single motion.

"Need some simple tools, too. Screwdriver; pair of pliers."

"Not gonna fix much with screwdriver, pliers and a six-pack of Bud!"

I've seen too much fixed with a screwdriver, pliers and a six-pack to ever take that kind of guff off a native down in Oklahoma. The Mustang still sat out on the flint-gravel apron. I caught glimpses of it in the passing headlights. Home, it almost seemed like home, my own home, a familiar place, a den, a nest, property, and I wondered if the yellowlegs had property. I fumbled in the dark with keys and fumbled in the dark with heater hose and clamps and filled the radiator with muddy water carried in a beer can from a tropical stream through red clay. I pulled off at a rest stop. I awoke to the sound of a great diesel engine idling beside and realized a trucker must also be resting, off on the dark turnoff. It was three in the morning. It would soon be gray in the tropics, and where I was heading one could not afford to arrive in the gray light of morning. Time to go, time to migrate, time to lowgrowl it own down that hiyuh-way to that one pond where the gray bird of fall would strut in the gray light of morning. The other side of that pond was Rockport. It was five hundred miles from the pond to Rockport, but had I known then of the impasse to come on the beach at Rockport, I might have stayed at the pond in the tropics. I had no permission to be at either place. You can go to Rockport without permission.

You can't go to the yellowlegs' pond without permission. Or without a key. You need both. It's a secure and secret place, on the outskirts of Norman, Oklahoma. Not many people know it's there. I know it's there, and a year ago I knew it was there. I've known for years of the secret yellowlegs pond on the outskirts of Norman. You don't come this far with a sandpiper to turn away just because you need a key and permission to go to the secret pond, do you? Of course not. When you know where you're going, and it's fall, and the whole world is migrating, you just go.

11 ⌐ To Touch a Yellowlegs

Wilkinson Weather
Local saying

*S*he was familiar with the sound of a gun, although her capacity for learning was not great, so she had never really figured out the connections between guns and the events that alarmed her. Her capacity for reaction *was* very great, however, so when that shotgun cracked the Kansas air, her unslotted primaries carried her a mile across the marshes. She could negotiate that mile in a minute if need be, and she could sort out, process, a thousand or million visual images in that minute. And upon it all her brain could rank those images in terms of genetically programmed sets of reactions, preferences, and the ranked images could then serve as a sieve data bank which fed muscles instructions. No American astronaut, settling a moon lander onto a dusty surface, computers churning, co-pilot hypercharged, blue flame licking an ancient satellite, adjustment after adjustment, reading after reading, by the foot, by the inch, down, down, down, touch; no, no American astronaut performing all those adjustments with the most technical society's most technical toy could ever come close to that of the machinery made by Nature. That performance out of machinery made by Nature occurred hundreds of times a day throughout the life of a gray bird that went from no-fly to fly within a fraction of a second after a shotgun exploded and pellets scattered in the grass around her.

She was gone; gone to the next pond where the last of the old-time naturalists looked her over with binoculars and decided she could be caught in a chicken-wire trap. Then she was gone again, gone to the southern edge of a great marsh where she acted agitated and twitty, then raised her wings, brought them down through the Kansas air and was gone for the season.

The wind whistled through her wings with each stroke, and she then entered as only she could that n-dimensional hyperexperience of rushing air, athletic endeavor and body control, sensory perception, with bare moist eyes into the fall wind and bare moist bill thrust in total confidence toward a place called Argentina. She flew south. The land clues gave her information. She processed that information with machinery that had been hers to use from the moment she'd entered the world through a mottled eggshell a few years before. And for the dirt-bound humans below, she had no feelings; they were only a part of her hyperexperience and in her mind the things they did only altered slightly her sequence of activities. In fact, the things they did altered her species' sequence of activities in ways she would never understand and could never communicate even if she understood. The world might as well have been going to hell; she was doing what her genes drove her to do and what her superb set of servomechanisms allowed her to do: migrate.

Beneath her a young boy "flew" a kite; paper and sticks and string drifting tethered on the prairie wind. She looked at the kite, for turning her head in flight was one of her options, but she did not know that the young boy considered his kite a magnificent achievement of design and construction that "flew" very well indeed! Beneath her on the outskirts of a city there "flew" a model airplane, powered by tiny alloy engine and tiny alloy gas tank holding tiny model fuel. Guided by the dials on a box held in the hands of an older boy, a box with an antenna, from which electronic workings sent tiny radio signals to tiny active mechanisms that turned flaps on wings and tails, the paper and wood and metal thing "flew" until it ran out of gas and landed, still under some kind of control. And this young man was proud of his flying toy and his ability to control it, and he was proud of his own ability to build and paint the things he "flew." She did not know that this young man also considered his radio-controlled airplane a magnificent achievement of design and construction that "flew" very well indeed. She saw the magnificent achievement land after a few hundred yards around some level ground. She continued after that on an eight-thousand-mile flight, round trip, during which she would fuel her wings with beetle larvae, never once would she be tethered by a string and during which she would encounter and deal with the plowed fields of an agriculturally crazed political entity, a rampaging industrial giant, the scarrings of lands as far as she could see and fly, the oils of Carboniferous disguised to look like the waters of life, a thousand miles of trackless Gulf, an equatorial forest of hummingbirds and Stone Age Indians, all for a few weeks of sunshine in a land called Argentina where people tried to kill her for food. She weighed less than the airplane and her wingspan was not as great.

Had she been philosophical, she might well have analyzed her mechanical abilities, her own function as a set of interworking parts, responding to signals from earth. She would have placed those abilities in some kind of perspective, one that included the *actual* abilities of man-made machines as well as man's opinions of his own skill at devising machines! Had she been derisive, she would have laughed at his feeble, but well-intentioned, attempts to invent and control machinery. Had she been elitest, she would have scorned man's stupidity that made him vulnerable to his own myopic pride and "needs"—"needs" that ripped apart her planet in the name of progress and made it uninhabitable for working parts that might well have been required before the Ultimate Machine would function properly. Had she been sensitive, she might have felt a twinge of regret that the two-legged ones over which she flew were depriving themselves of their finest heritage by the very acts of supplying their bodily needs. That sensitivity might have sprung from the fact that she had no higher needs beyond those of supplying her perfect functions, and thus was in a position to see the tragedy of a species that *had* higher needs, yet so often ignored those higher needs, and so sought only to supply the bodily needs and wants. And had she been easily depressed, she would have been mightily discouraged that the two-legged ones had allowed themselves to become slaves to machines that hardly merited the name, in comparison to her own body.

Had she been intellectual, she would have extended that discouragement to include the attitude that actually considered man's finest machines *fine,* in comparison to her own body. And had she been religious, she might well have considered man's slavery to his machines, his tangible machines of working parts as well as his *intangible* political machines and bureaucracies of working parts, the ultimate sin against man's creative potential. And had she been rebellious and irreverent, she would have seen the Master Mechanic's attitude toward all this machinery, her own included, as the only attitude which would in the end preserve the human dignity with which every one of the two-legged ones was hatched but which was so often denied them so early in their fledging. And had she been a biologist, she would have spent many hours wondering just how best to convey that romantic approach of a Master Mechanic to thousands of fledglings who would so soon, like her and her own young, encounter the Technological State. But of course she was none of these things. She was simply a bird. She didn't even know I was following her for some reason of my own, intent upon becoming the ultimate ecologist, perhaps as a feeble attempt to convey that romantic approach of some Master Mechanic for the Ultimate Machine. She knew and felt none of this I've just dreamed. Instead, she cruised into that territory, the one I've called the Tropics, where the land was blood-red and the people below her did interesting things.

On the land below lay great ribbons of concrete and steel that stretched out over the prairie as far as she could see from any height, and she followed these ribbons from time to time, not knowing or caring that the people below were paying so foreign a concept as "money" for the privilege of being on those ribbons. She had never been exposed to money or barter, or permission, and the things she built were of total simplicity and natural materials. She had never stopped because of another species, or species-equivalent, or because of some rule written way back in a book, nor had she ever limited her speed because of any rule other than those in her own genes. She chose her route and her speed and her manner and her stopping places, but she did not choose the fact of her journey. And in this most fundamental of ways she remained wild, so different from the strugglers below her. So few, so very few of them had ever been told by any power, be it their own elected or the societies within which they lived, that their only task was to perform those functions most characteristic of their species, that no rules or regulations would be placed on their efforts and that if they succeeded, their species would survive.

She flew over oil, but of course knew nothing of oil, or the oil bidniss, or the oil bidniss service bidniss, nor of the oil bidniss finance bidniss, nor of the history of boom and bust, a lifetime's money poured into a ragged hole in the earth, nor, so far luckily, of the ponds that looked like water from the air but turned out to be traps, heavy, penetrating, that devastated the will of a wild thing soaked with oil or petroleum waste. Below her silent powerful menial pumping units nodded away their useful lives to the puttering rhythm of a small gas engine and the rolling-eyed gaze of cattle. The menials forever nodded their heads, in agreement across the land, finishing up the gut work behind dashing explorers, the cutting rigs, swearing men, and *diamonds* on a bit to cut to the center of the earth. Sometimes the menials nodded in synchrony, sometimes not. They waited in donkey patience while service people in pickups jounced across an overgrazed red field to pull out their tubes. All the excitement had gone to the explorers. It would always go to the explorers. Even a dry hole was exciting, a gamble, usually with someone else's money, and although the drillers almost always got paid, they were still disappointed when their efforts went for naught. Even the best of strikes was thrown at the feet of the pumpers, however, while rigs and *diamond* bits went off looking for more. She flew above, knowing only what her senses told her— that somehow the world had become complex.

She had never studied humans, thus had no criteria upon which to age them, or sex them, or determine their ecological relation- ships or food habits, and she would never live long enough to learn of their history. Had she been able to age some of those below her, however, she would have known that the older ones were alive when this rebel land's psyche was established. The land was red so it was given to red people. Then it had been taken away and taken away in a manner that would forever burn in the minds and attitudes of these human animals. A line was drawn on the land and the animals waited until noon, when the shot of a gun set them off forever across the line and down the road to diversity, riches, poverty, welfare, scandal, sweet smug success and failure that was as often sneered at as bemoaned. "Here it is, take it!" had said some official, and "take it" they did and would forever. They even openly admired the ones that rebelled against the line, so slipped across and got what they thought was the best. And so admired were those that rebelled against the line that they and all their descendents after them called themselves "Sooners," and were generally proud of it. But she was just a bird, beautiful physical machine of simple requirements, and concepts such as "best" were not part of her equipment.

If she knew nothing of the "best" then she of course knew nothing of the "worst," and even less of the "best" that turned out to be "worst" and the "worst" that turned out to be very good indeed. She had never seen how land that couldn't grow corn, or wheat, or support cattle, or cotton, had a way of sprouting oil instead. She had never seen a weathered lean ole boy tryin' to raise up four kids with no muther on a dirt patch watch the machinery roll into that patch and make him a millionaire, him leanin' on a blackjack faints post figurn sum day pull thit wyar tat sos them cattle cain't get at but all that time grinnin' out side of mouth with cracked lips at the stack of black pipe 'cumulatin' up in thit rig, black pipe with a *diamond* on the tip to probe the Carboniferous for gold. Stuff like that had a way of remindin' folks that there *were* options in life, that one didn't *always* have to endure a role foisted off on them by some system.

So in a very real sense she shared much with the ant people below her. Nature had told her only to do the best with what she had, leave no twig unturned to find that larva. Nature of some kind had said something similar to those below her, had told them there were no restrictions on their use of their own abilities to scratch out a living in the tropics, and that psyche was still alive and well. Wheat and cotton were nice, and even in some cases a person should have outright reverence for wheat and cotton. But big oil had a way

127

of putting wheat and cotton into perspective. So the tropical animals grew up in an environment in which *perspective* was an ecological heritage. That heritage, that ecological heritage, a human result of diversity, would serve them well; as well, perhaps, as a yellowlegs' wings.

The irreverence that allowed a nickname like "Sooner" with all its implications had spawned some other monumental types. There was a twirling fumble-mouthed cowboy who made shambles of pomposity, patronage, ritual for the sake of ritual, and second-handers who used their own talents for no other purpose than to milk the bloodwork of others. The ecological diversity was great, of course, so the fumble-mouthed cowboy's approach to life underwent many modifications, but it remained recognizable, almost as a species character of these people. (Jist 'cawse guvvamint says it don't mean it's *so*; rat?) But the irreverence for rules extended to the *natural* rules that often govern relationships between animals and the places they live. So when the winds came and the rain stopped, the habitat quickly became uninhabitable, and some of the tropical animals left, migrating far to the west, where they acquired another nickname, this one not so proud. In retrospect, any biologist could have guessed what would happen: the ecological diversity spawned still another talent and heritage of monumental proportions. He rode trains and wrote songs and finally died of a strange disease, he got in a lot of trouble but he had a lot to say, and the Okie people never had much trouble after that accepting creative thinking, creative doing, creative drinking and carousing, or creative play.

The diverse tropical culture may not, in the final analysis, have actually *created* the soft spoken tall handsome young articulate disarming smiling silver haired genius that came walking into the country one day with a pittance salary. But the diverse tropical culture did create the *opportunity* for this last of the tall-in-the-saddle men from out of the sunset to take the land by its handle in one hand and its heart in the other and make it his. The fumble-mouthed cowboy's irreverence, culturally inherited from those who slipped across a line, broken through the surface in songs of a land gone tough, manifest even in the attitude of an elderly woman shopping in the core of a city gone decrepit, manifest itself again in the thoughts and deeds of this silver hero. It was all right to be the best. Most of all it was all right to use one's brains to become the best, even if one became best in war games not everyone associated with brains. They put the silver one in charge of their play army and sent the army across the land to do war. And do war it did. The silver one thought about ways to place his soldiers behind and along the lines, translated his thoughts into zeros and X's for his staff to see on a blackboard, taught those thoughts to young men, dressed those young soldiers in red and white and plastic, sent them into an arena, and paced the sidelines while they acted out his theatrics to the crazed hosannas of their parents.

Small wonder that this land should also have produced a Master Mechanic with an irreverence for rules, a romantic in a classics' business, with an ultimate respect for the "feel" of a machine. And she the gray bird of night flew into all this through the dark, her own body a machine of sorts, responding to the celestial ballet of her planet The Ultimate Machine, for her rendezvous with a ragged biologist, himself a ragged machine with grease underneath his fingernails, waiting with a sense of mission at a secret pond, waiting to touch her if he could.

She finally saw her place in the middle of all this madness. It was a place she had visited twice a year for all the few years of her life and it was a place she would visit this day. Its location had been published in a national journal, but one read only by initiates, so it was still a safe place. She came to her place in the evening, last light of a fall Friday turning old gray asphalt into deeper gray, grasses of cracks in that asphalt whipping stiffly in the cool prairie wind. The water lapped over the corner of an airfield, from a farmer's small dammed stream. A half a mile away the personal and executive private jets screamed in with cocktails for tomorrow's war; sandpipers and meadowlarks gathered on the unused corner. On her first visit to this place she had chased small things in the water and watched two thirds of the world's population of buff-breasted sandpipers come and go from the water's edge. She had no way of knowing, but a special place like that would always, *always,* catch the eye of some biologist.

The swirling Oklahoma diversity generated a sense of need at times, in both man and beast, a need for quiet and peace. It also generated places and times where that need could be filled. And it generated people like biologists and birds like yellowlegs that would find those places and meet in them. She set her wings in a long glide. There were others there and some were beginning to sleep out in the shallow water. She waded out a few yards. Her muscles ached and she had not yet even considered the Gulf of Mexico. The night passed with prairie sounds as well as traffic, semi-trailers a mile away whining to pass, Plymouth jacked up rear end whining on a city street after Tiger game. The dawn came with teal, whistling in from the west, gray light with coffee smell from the east, and the sound of a band practicing somewhere to the south. She opened her eyes and gazed at the car parked in the willows and tall grass. She preened with an eye on the human only a few yards away with binoculars trained on her very soul. She went about her business; there were small things in the water to be eaten.

That whole day there were small things in the water to be eaten, eaten while a ragged man lay on a bank between young willows and a couple of red earth ridges and watched. She and the others paid him little attention except at first. At first she watched back this strange animal, but its posture and context paralanguage told her "harmless." Posture and context, remember, are the interspecies medium, the universal animal language. The inner serenity stemming from possession, even if for only a day, of a place in the dirt beside an airfield's corner, a place where yellowlegs gathered and could be watched at close range, completely controlled this human's body. He could only communicate "harmless." So the bird worked her way around the edge, sidestepping with a wary tilt of her head a small flock of pectorals, tensing every time a killdeer cried "wolf," until she found herself on the same side as that hulk in the grass with binoculars. She went about her business, rested now, and oblivious to the sounds of a Saturday athletic war drifting out across the land, carried by the slight breeze to where a man lay in the grass and red dirt and understood everything.

Still she worked closer, and the man smiled, but across the land came a muffled roar of frustration and an angry roar of disapproval in quick succession. Still she poked along the bank closer to the man, but across the plains came the sounds of brass music. Each step brought her closer to the man lying in the grass, while across the roads far to the south came the sounds of gunfire, and a few seconds later more gunfire, the blood lust roars of human mobs and martial music that screamed and pleaded for more gunfire. She heard none of this, none of it registered; he heard it all. She sensed none of the importance of all this, while he sensed all of the loneliness of a scientist intent upon his curiosity and love at a time the rest of the world was doing something else. The war continued unabated until late afternoon, and by then she was close enough to see him continuously. She was almost as close as she had ever been to a human and regardless of his communication, she could not help tensing slightly, then more, then backing off slightly, as she came closer and she could see his attention develop. He tried mightily to remain calm and silent, but his insides with his yellowlegs *this close* would not let him. They were almost touching now, she ankle deep in the water, drawn in some way she could not understand to this spot where lay a human, and he, dirty and unkempt in the grass, heart pounding dangerously for a man of forty, hoping against what he had always known was all hope, that the bird would actually come to him. A wild thing, a thing so wild no words or picture could ever convey that wildness, and a thing so fragile none except those that had killed such a thing could ever understand, was this yellowlegs.

She stood in the water at his shoulder now and stared into a face that could only have belonged to this person at this time. The scientist at *his* moment, his moment of confrontation with the object of his pursuit, almost touching, not quite, was this man. This scientist at the moment of confrontation with the object of his pursuit was totally out of communication with the war world and the rest of his species drinking yelling driving fast cars chasing women spending money doing play-by-play over and over again across the street up and down the street in homes in apartments with smug glee and exploding confidence that someone was number one in every home in land with small children red sweat shirts size extrasmall dad and mom going out to party next week's opponent big time had by all back to every conceivable job on Monday after an afternoon with Dallas cheerleaders on tube while this man in the pasture simply watched, and experienced, and for the precious

131

moments of a biologist with his animal, did nothing but look at the live bird at his shoulder. She was not afraid. She was a little suspicious, tensing slightly, when this human held out his hand with a few insect larvae, and she made a move to take them from his hand, but something pulled her head back and she couldn't do it. The expression on his face changed slightly, his hand so gently extended further toward her, and again she made a move to take the larvae from his hand, but again she could not do it. He turned suddenly then, frightened, almost terrified, it seemed to her, to the east, and the sounds of an approaching engine and a jouncing metal vehicle spurted through the willows. She was gone then, across the pond, where she settled to watch.

It was a blue and white vehicle, with machinery and lights on top, and she sensed that this moving thing was somehow different from the wild Mustang parked in the field. This human's posture and communications changed, they no longer said "harmless and serene," and she was afraid now, afraid of the man from whom she had almost taken food. Two others, large ones, emerged from the new machine and walked toward the scientist, hands on their hips where they carried some other machines. The three talked together, her ragged human pointing at her out over the water, then pointing repeatedly to the pectorals and killdeer then back to her. His hands moved excitedly, and the sounds of his voice carried out across the water. The three walked to the stray Mustang, then back to the water. The talking became very much louder now, and her scientist's behavior became very interesting, communicating many kinds of things she'd never known, frustrations, emotions. He still pointed to her and offered his binoculars to the new men. She saw them shaking their heads until finally one of them took her man by the arm and led him away into the new vehicle. They were all gone then, and she had a faint sense of something missing, something different. It was still later, almost toward evening of a perfect fall day, when still another vehicle came jouncing across the fields. This one was large, and when it left, the small white car followed it closely, one end raised un-naturally high. These were all very different experiences for a thing so wild no words or tale could ever describe that wildness. She became very nervous, sensing, feeling with no reason exactly the way some Master Mechanic might have felt something wrong with some automobile for no reason, that something was wrong with her pond.

She had no knowledge or understanding of a *concept* such as a rule that said one could not drive across an air field to get to the corner of an old runway and park there for days. No body politic had ever told her she could not stop at this place for as long as the Earth signs told her it was safe. Nor could she understand the *concept* of a rule that said a living thing could not go when and where that living thing desired, governed only by a set of genes, including travels of the mind as well as streamsides and pond edges. What she had just witnessed was a human event, an event that said a human could not be at this place where shorebirds gathered, unless he had permission that no shorebird ever had. She had also just witnessed a human event that said having *come* to a shorebird place without permission, one could now not *leave* without permission. What she had just witnessed was the fate of a scientist operating alone in his mind far away from the dehumanizing routine of being human in the technological state, the serenity and all-consuming love of that scientist at his moment of encounter with the wild and unknown, the serious attempts by that scientist to convey that serenity to ones who didn't know sandpipers, and then failure in those attempts.

Ah, machinery! Machinery with red lights atop, machinery bought used from Pops back in Kansas a trillion miles into history, engines that drink gas, engines that need bugs, machines that fly the night skies, machines of steel, machines of feathers, Lonnie, alternators, heater hoses, equipment, yes, ah yes, *equipment, equipment* is the word, is it not, for the appurtenances of the technological condition? How our matrix fields all intersect! What a failure my feeble attempt to act like an animal, to leave that Mustang, symbol of my nation, my culture, the intellectual environment that spawned me, and crawl through the dirt with insect larvae to a sandpiper! Rockport; there remained a year ago only Rockport by the sea. Would I have gone to Rockport, knowing the impasse that lay there for me on the beach? Would I hve gone onward from Norman, would I have lain in that cell still with my hand held clutching insect larvae, had I known of the beach at Rockport? Of course. Migratory animals do what they must! They make few purposeful decisions; they just go. Go! Follow the wild avenue into a future.

The Norman, Oklahoma, city jail is the absolute pits. There were drunks, and they puked all over everything and it reeked with sour acid smell of half-digested alcohol, then they stepped around in that puke and stumbled against the walls and yelled out slurred language and cops spoke back in slurred language and it was all the pits. The mighty Sooners had whipped up unmercifully on the hapless Kansas State Wildcats that afternoon, that much I got out of my night in jail; the football scores. I tried to talk to a few of those people down there; they never understood my language. There must be something about the nouns and verbs of natural history that make them sound slurred and incoherent in places like the Norman, Oklahoma, city jail. Somewhere out there was my car, my *equipment*. Somewhere out there they were bending my bumper; it happens every time a car is towed by someone other than a Master Mechanic. You all know that. They'll screw up your transmission, too, if they get the chance. It gets hopeless in a hurry in the Norman city jail, especially when you're from Nebraska and it's football season and you're talking a language nobody understands and you're driving a car that's not licensed yet and you've driven that car across the Norman city airport runway. I don't know why these kinds of people take things so seriously. They don't know about the sandpipers out there, do they. I tried to tell them, offered one of those brutes my binocs. Didn't do much good. Not much entertainment for a Nebraskan in the Norman city jail during football season, especially if you're a scientist. I spent the night doing some evaluation of this task of doing my kind of work and decided it might be more difficult than I at first envisioned. I suspect that bird out there on the runway didn't like this turn of events either. They probably spelled some strange things about her airfield. I'm sure she flew straight to the Gulf of Mexico where her internal regulatory mechanisms and genes would tell her it was permitted to stay and gather strength for a flight across a trackless ocean and a just as trackless jungle.

My bumper *was* bent. I stood staring, eyes adjusting to the bright afternoon Oklahoma sun, blinking, wondering about a screwed up transmission, but I never felt a need to stay in Oklahoma to gather strength for a dash across a trackless ocean and a just as trackless jungle called Texas. I didn't know it at the time, but I was headed for Rockport. Rockport; I shake my head slowly, nowadays, when I hear that word: Rockport.

12 ⌐ Rockport

Burnet, his wife and several members
of the Texas cabinet were only a few yards
offshore in Galveston Bay when Santa Anna's
dragoons clattered up.

David Nevin

I drove with a vengeance then, across a river so appropri-
ately named "Red," and was welcomed by a concrete state, a new
gray/brown/yellow land, and a new set of rules. I started my
acceleration mid-bridge, but as I hit the line was still passed within
a quarter mile by a large General Motors product with Texas tags,
antennas whipping. I drove with the anger that this sort of
atmosphere would allow, an atmosphere where everyone went as
fast as everyone could and the outsider felt all the more outside
because he didn't really understand what was going on. I pointed
my machine to the south and again pushed on the floor to hear the
valves burn and know I was putting pain into the steel muscles of a
faithful servant. There were a million places to go, a million
choices, and I had no idea where to even begin thinking. I had not
even so much as a direction, for one does not make a sighting on
yellowlegs' flight from the dismal innards of a college town jail.
The sum total of that business made me furious then, and the anger
had not subsided in the miles that followed—the anger at the
enormity of a task about which I had set so seriously. It all soared
out of proportion, this driving and *thinking,* but still I pushed my
pedal to the floor and hung on the sides of curves and ran the

million choices through my mind again and again as I hurtled toward a city where a President had been shot in the head, where a stoic soldier innovated cheerleaders, and where I had once seen the *owner* of a packing plant standing in work clothes at the sausage machine making sure he knew the bidniss.

The coast passed before my eyes, with continuous evaluation, as a film strip in head's projector, and in every frame there was a gray sandpiper, then there was no gray sandpiper, then the images were compared and evaluated so that the particular frame was retained or cast aside. They ran from a soggy eastern heavily industrialized coast, Navy and Marines and PT boats, tankers, refineries, things painted gray, oil on the waters, to the sanctuaries of Copano Bay and Rockport to the crystal stretch of Padre Island to Aransas Pass with screaming gulls, royal terns, between a trillion miles of scrub live oak, rattlesnakes, human as well as reptilian, boats, mostly decrepit except for the Southern Ocean Racing Conference out of Houston, shrimp in a beat-up town at the end of a long beat-up road, oysters in a quart cardboard ice cream container, as everywhere gulls, laughing gulls, *Larus atricilla,* calling, twisting turning gliding wings set picking snapping biting argue bluff graybacked and reflective white, purest of white white reflecting a land, below gulls. But where in all this mess to find a yellowlegs? Where does a small machine rest for a few days before a routine "considerable migration at sea?" I was south of Dallas then, decision time, so with all the total frustration of one who knows full well he might be wrong, I turned toward a place called Rockport and drove still angry, still pounding inside with my failure at public relations back at the edge of a small worthless pond, and I noticed as the light faded and the night stayed warm that there were still insects out in this territory. They hit the windshield, sometimes hard. The heavy ones must have been grasshoppers.

There had been a time many years ago when I had once before walked those beaches and driven those back roads, the roads of Rockport and Copano Bay, in and out of a personal wildlife preserve and foundation with Spanish buildings where at the time I wanted simply to stay. I had seen a "Keep Out" sign on private property and had seen a "Birdwatchers Welcome" sign on that same personal property. Well, that was great! Birdwatcher I was then and birdwatcher I was now, and it was great as all living hell to know that somewhere down there I would be welcome! I had seen the skimmers at those times past, out birdwatching, had stood transfixed as they actually did what they were supposed to do, what all my pictures back home in books had shown them to do, but still I had been transfixed by the real thing. It was only later, many years later, that I reflected back on the skimmer experience, back on the value of the real thing. One *knew* a skimmer flew like that, one had *seen* it in a Walt Disney film about water birds, set to appropriate music, and one had been *shown* with slow motion the unique wing movements of a skimmer feeding over the surface, blinking up fish with a twist of the neck, a high-powered all fast air knife soft prying flutter above shoulder height skimming flight movements for a skimmer. But to stand on the shores of Rockport and actually see the real thing, alive and well and functioning, was an experience that left me hypnotized for a great long time. I never saw as much in the real thing alive as I had seen in the pictures, but then I had *felt* things in the presence of the real thing that I had never felt in the presence of the imitations.

I extended that line of skimmer thought in later years to include all things experienced in representation as opposed to experienced in *real,* and thus, I suppose, when it came time to experience the yellowlegs, living *its* life to the best of my ability, in contact with *it,* was the only valid answer. But when it came time to *teach* the yellowlegs, when it came time to convey the feel of a functioning earth that only a life with sandpipers could ensure, then I stumbled on clay feet, and had many times walked into a classroom with two hundred eager faces, stepped to the rostrum, and fully prepared to deliver golden words of wisdom, had said to myself, "What am I doing here?" I was the medium through which the yellowlegs and all other functioning living parts of a planet were supposed to be represented to the next generation. So I delivered my lectures and thought about skimmers and yellowlegs and nearly cried with a desire to take each one of the two hundred to the river for a lesson in reality. And when it was all over they thought they had *learned* and I told my boss I'd been *teaching,* but I always knew that both thoughts and statements were not true. These were the things in my mind that night as I aimed my second-hand car toward

Rockport where once in the distant past I had seen the skimmers.

I was on a scientific expedition the last time we drove along the beach into Rockport, a scientific expedition to determine many unknown facts about creatures such as yellowlegs and dowitchers. The expeditionary force made many discoveries indeed, interesting and valuable discoveries, although I later received some criticism. I had killed a yellowlegs, perhaps more than one. I could see even then the lines of thought leading from that act to one of many conclusions. One of those lines of thought said a yellowlegs should not be killed, that all of the observations could be made without actually putting the bird down with a shotgun. But such a line of thought extended into the future and ended up two places. One such place said a total respect for the life of a wild thing should govern and set the limits to human investigation of that wild thing. The other place said there were certain areas of unknown that should not be explored. As I began breathing once more south of Dallas, I concluded that the first of these places where such lines of thought led was still alive and well in the minds of those dealing with such esoteric items of culture as bald eagles and California condors. The second of the places, to which led lines of thought, was also alive and well, but in the minds of men like one Senator Proxmire, perpetrator of the "Golden Fleece" award, and men who made out budgets, and men who tried to "govern and manage" great institutions whose *mission, ultimate mission,* was to leave no area of ignorance unchallenged. It did not bother me a year ago that I had killed the yellowlegs as a student. I had made my discoveries then. I had participated in the headiest of human activities: adult original science. And I had come away different from the rest. These were the things in my mind that night as I aimed my second-hand car toward Rockport where I had once in the distant past killed the yellowlegs.

I read somewhere that Rockport has the longest list of resident and transient birds of any spot in the nation and that persons come from afar to add Rockport's residents and transients to *their own* lists, life lists. I tried mightily once to collect a "life list," but after a few years failed and gave up. Then in my own special way, inherited perhaps, I rationalized that failure with a self-generated conclusion about life lists. I simply decided, for what I felt were excellent and valid reasons, that the accumulation of a long life list in the absence of a serious love and experience with a single name on the list was a worthless activity. In this way the accumulation of a long life list became the equivalent of the accumulation of a long *life*. The decision to explore in all possible depth the implications of any one name on that life list became the equivalent of experiencing a rich and full life, regardless of how long. So when both my parents died brutal withering malignant deaths while still in their prime, I looked back on *their* life lists and decided that in their short lives they had taken more and given more than most and had done things and thought thoughts that most members of the human gene pool either could not or would not, so when they left, they left more and took more than any birdwatcher with only long life and long life list. Then when Glenn died also, I was ready. I extracted the *quality* and *meaning* from what Glenn had done and stood for and finally decided that in the message of *meaning* and *quality*, Glenn lived on in eternity. That message said, when once passed through the river and a bird's body, that the planet was a beautiful machine of incredible complexity and infinite working parts with established but upon occasion flexible relationships with one another, and that one species had no business making the Classic's mistake of letting inferior machines, both steel and political, both electrical and engineerical, as well as the attendant machine-like *thinking*, ultimately destroy this *most* magnificent machine, when in fact what was required to prevent such destruction was a touch of the Romantic. A touch of the feel, a touch of the sense, a willingness to act on the sense and feel, with perhaps no supporting *facts* or *arguments* or *convincing reasons*, other than the ones that said there are things on this planet that are worthy and should be respected as such on an equal with humanity, that's what Glenn ultimately said was required. These were the thoughts in my mind, right or wrong, that night as I aimed my second-hand car at Rockport where I had once in the distant past refused to continue my life list and instead had chosen to be transfixed by the skimmers.

The last trip to Rockport and other places along the Texas coast was great fun, although there were plenty of those back home who thought at the time that any kind of science that was great fun was perhaps not valid science. I have seen much of science in the years since that Texas trip and have done much of science, have suffered all the frustrations and elations of science, have spent the money of science and tried to teach the finds of science. Now that it's all said and done, I have concluded that science is the purest form of adult entertainment but that in many ways science is similar to chasing women. I cannot think of any other job except that of a scientist, which in its purest form exists *only* for the purpose of stepping into the new and unknown. In every case the new and unknown are areas of the mind. Thus the business about women. Most of the excitement is in the idea; most of the entertainment value in this purest form of adult entertainment is in consideration of the unknown. There are always some initial experiments to be conducted, no matter what the idea, and there is always *some* satisfaction to be had from an initial experiment that actually works and yields. Then there is the problem of validation, publication, rituals of the formal business of science. The experiments have to be repeated and repeated and finally formalized and made public as formalized and repeated experiments, experiments which everyone assumes have been done in the privacy of some laboratory in order to validate for all time that which was once new and unknown. And all the while more new and unknown ideas, teasing possibilities, walk the streets and bars of the fertile mind, waiting, just waiting, seemingly, for an initial experiment to start the process once again! These were the things in my mind as I aimed my second-hand car through the night toward Rockport where once in the distant past I had great fun doing science.

I was but a "student" on my last trip to Rockport, and not a very good one at that, there being much at the time that I didn't really know about. But I was treated with respect by fellow professionals, taking turns driving a government vehicle, and some of these professionals were *teachers,* men advanced far ahead of me and men who would ultimately advance even farther. But they treated me as an equal. It all went back to a philosophy, or an approach, that was used on me very early in my career: assume the student is a professional the moment the decision is made to pursue a career, then place upon that student's shoulders all the burdens of professionalism in the chosen field, then see if the student makes it!

The self-esteem that accompanies such treatment by obvious superiors, sometimes scientists of truly world renown, is a self-esteem that carries one through many rough places over the years. Maybe I had begun my sabbatical that day knowing it was one way for me to validate what for me is a known fact: students are to be treated as equals, professionals, and no matter who the student, the objectivity, love, feel, sense, interest, pride, value—all things the teacher has that keeps him moving in the subject area—are to be imparted, conveyed, discussed, and even when things get technical, as often they do, that love and sense of value in one's chosen work should still prevail. The rituals of power and politics and business have to be thrown out when one begins teaching, for as in science itself, the norms of business and politics constitute corruption when applied to a teaching/learning situation. These were the things on my mind that night as I drove my second-hand car to its limits toward Rockport where once in the distant past I had been a student.

I had learned things on my last trip to Rockport, and not only did I learn things but I learned how to learn things and how to *do* things, how to generate thoughts, and how to sustain a life of learning, and ultimately how to judge oneself more harshly and critically than others could ever do. My role on the Rockport trip was to bring back information about animals. New information. The assumption that such information could be had was based only on things printed in books and estimates which were thought-extensions of things printed in books. I planned my time and money and clothing for the expedition, and in so doing learned a little about the logistics of original science. I stood beside a senior scientist as that person collected valuable animals for scientific purposes and begged the innards and carcasses of those animals, and in so doing learned how to extract *all* the information from a collected animal. I had little trouble after that accepting the yellowlegs as a community when I met myself on a Kansas dike. The last Rockport trip was not a total success, but then it was not a total failure either. There was some information of value which was collected, some information that added a concept to a picture building in the mind of my employer at the time, but that information was not necessarily what my employer thought would derive from the expedition. My employer accepted the information as a new and equal friend, for in science practice it certainly was. So I studied things on that expedition I was not "required" to study, and painted pictures of animals, and borrowed carcasses, and generally made a nuisance of myself, but brought back some information and some paintings.

The Rockport paintings are among my very best. And when I returned from Rockport that last time, I told of all my experiences, all the things I had learned, showed the paintings to my wife and an expert painter and teacher, and generally spent many days after that in a state of euphoria from having been to Rockport and done things on my own and studied things I didn't have to study. Even the paintings, those were not "required" of me; they were done just to record for my own use in my own way the experiences of Rockport. The expert had looked over my paintings and nodded smiling, and commented on a few things that were "done very well indeed." So in the years after Rockport I took more of my paintings to this highly successful and skillful man, and each time the man took the paintings, went through them carefully, and chose one or two to talk about, then picked out in those one or two the very things, even single details, which were done properly. Quite by accident I discovered after almost twenty years of all this treatment exactly how it was I was being treated! The experts I have learned the most from, the ones that influenced me the most when I was only learning, and the ones who were also world figures in their own rights at the time, were always ones who picked out what I did right, then dwelt upon that "right" deed. In the end, having discovered this biased treatment, I also discovered that the positive support of recognizing only that which was done satisfactorily and ignoring that which was done incorrectly was in the long run the very thing that sustained me in my chosen field of endeavor. Quickly I learned how to judge myself more harshly. Pick out that part of one's own work which a world expert would admit was done properly and be confident in that decision. Pick out that part of one's own work that a world expert who was also a *teacher* would probably ignore, and that was the part that needed repetition with modification. These were the things in my mind that night as I drove my second-hand car toward Rockport, where I had once in the distant past studied things I did not have to study.

On the last trip to Rockport, the route was circuitous. I can't remember whether we went to Rockport before or after Padre Island. I can remember well the quart of oysters we cooked. I can also remember very well standing on the bluffs above a place called Copano Bay, not far from Rockport, and watching the shorebirds below. I remember very well driving into that town and deciding that Rockport was no different from just outside Rockport. I remember it as a place of old and retired people, and have thought many times of those years ahead when I myself will "retire," and I have wondered whether I should retire to live in Rockport. Most of Texas seemed boring then, especially the part on the way to Rockport, but I have been to Texas many many times and never found it boring, so I always wonder why it was boring along *that* highway, when in fact I have nothing but the most exciting memories of Texas. My mind became the blur it normally does out on the highway for long periods, and the lights and towns and used machinery and grasshoppers of a southern night swept by, gradually being replaced by graying scudding clouds of southern dawn, down in a part of the world where the air smelled of salt, the laughing gulls still called, and the cars were rusted. Dark children stood waiting for a schoolbus. Mechanics in clean but worn clothes carried lunch pails down the streets and sidewalks of a small town. Dogs trotted alongside a concrete highway, sidestepping rain puddles. Live oaks, twisted, and miles of scrub came right up to the shoulder and every plant looked prickly. Roads led off into the trees toward the coast. A highway sign proclaimed ROCKPORT. These were the things I saw that early morning as I returned in search of the banded yellowlegs to a place called Rockport.

My head hurt very badly. My anger at the time spent with policemen, jerked from the most idyllic and loving moment when I *knew* the bird was about to feed from my hand, crept to the surface from its smoldering pocket inside. My breathing became more deep. I was as tired as I ever have been, and my stomach and back were killing me. I was old, old as all time, and my clothes were dirty, at land's end, and there were beach houses where I wanted to go, and the coast did not look at all like I thought it should at a place I remembered as Rockport, the actual place where water met land and my yellowlegs should be. I had this sense of my bird having become a Texas citizen, a member of a clique which did not include me. I had a sense of impending considerable migration at sea of which I was not a part. So I wormed my still straining Mustang through the back coastal streets of Rockport until I came to the place where the breakwater went a ways out into the ocean and the oystershell road sort of splayed out over the beach and led to an ocean that I was not sure anyone would want to swim in and there I saw a small flock, loose flock along the moving water's edge below the tide line, totally absorbed in what they were doing, small loose flock of yellowlegs; and some smaller things that I did not bother to try to identify, and a couple of skimmers out over the Gulf, and the laughing gulls, and it was all very tranquil, and serious, in the gray light of morning, as I sat blood pressure mounting heart pounding while my windshield wipers slowly cleared the haze and mist and my binoculars searched the flock for the ankle bracelet.

The wind picked up slightly, then more strongly, and a boat tied out on a dock began to pitch, and small breakers began to come in as the sky darkened slightly. The birds became wary and stopped their feeding. I had still not seen a band. They moved in loose synchrony now, first this way and then that for short distances along the shore as the breakers ran further up on the sand. The smaller things left first, almost as a unit the entire flock hesitated then was gone, passing across my field of vision with a cutting of wings that told of a regular and considerable migration at sea even for these small ones. I knew it was time then. The yellowlegs did the same, lifting gently, peeling off from the sand into the ocean wind that was now driving scattered drops against the windows on the other side of the car. I knew nothing at the time, I only sensed and felt, from some combination of behaviors and actions, that they were gone and would not see land again for some time. I had no control over myself then. I would only remember the water later; I would not remember turning the key; I would not remember my eyes squinting burning fixed through the rain at the place where water and land met; I would not remember my engine straining as I twisted my mouth and put the car in gear and aimed it toward the disappearing flock of yellowlegs.

The white Mustang hit the surf with a roar and a rush of steam from a scalded steel engine as I sat still staring from a window. Breakers came in over the hood and blurred my vision along with the driving rain. I later remembered the water. It crept in and before long was up to my waist inside the car. A Budweiser can floated out from under the seat and tinkled cheerfully and comfortingly against the steering column. I never looked back at that automobile in the surf. I counted wet money as I walked back up towards the highway, wet through with salt water, its taste on my hands as I wiped the rain from my face. There were twenty-one dollars in my envelope, twenty-one dollars of good American money. I stopped in front of an older woman in rain gear and binoculars and fished in my wet pocket for change, which I counted as she smiled at me.

"Gone, aren't they?"

"Seventeen cents. Twenty-one dollars and seventeen cents." My binoculars still swung from my neck.

"Gone, aren't they?" she repeated, still smiling.

"I was following that bird."

"I could tell. Sometimes they leave for good this week, sometimes next week, never can tell, but it always happens within this couple of weeks. Way they were acting, I'd say they're gone until spring. Seen it many times, live right up here off the highway, and I've seen it many times before since we moved down here. Sandpipers just decide one day it's time to go and they're off. Who knows where and which way they go. They'll be back, mostly in March. They're gone for now, son, gone until spring."

"Were any of them banded?"

"Couldn't tell from way up here. Would really surprise me if a sandpiper was banded. Don't get your hands on a sandpiper very often to band it!"

I stood looking for a time out over the Gulf, shivering slightly in the coastal fall wind, still wet and salt beginning to prickle my skin beneath stiff jeans and Gulf sand.

"Have a good day!" I said. I was not able to bring myself to talk biology to this old lady at this particular time. I had total confidence in my decision that she probably did not need it. I took my first steps north, back toward the highway.

"Give you a ride somewhere?"

"Yeah, lady; I'm goin' back to Nebraska!" I grinned now.

"Well, I was just on my way down for a bottle of vodka, but I could take you to Nebraska!"

"I can tell you a story on the way."

"I bet you can!"

"Stop for the vodka anyway?"

"Sure. Now where to exactly in Nebraska?"

And this is how it happened that I discovered in my most technical society to have ever evolved in the human race that I did not have the equipment nor the technical skills to follow the yellowlegs that day in Rockport. In the years that come I will always try to discover in my own mind exactly what it would take to follow the yellowlegs, and I suspect I will always conclude that the wild things can do stuff no human can do or can ever hope to do, and that the wild things do this stuff routinely. I know that many years from now these will still be the things in my mind as I aim my thoughts at Rockport, where I once tried to follow the yellowlegs across the Gulf of Mexico.

13 ∽ In Bed

Zoology seems much more practical in a swamp.

Anonymous student

The first spatters of sleet were hitting the early-night sidewalks and driveways when I turned the final corner and stepped across my own front yard toward my own front door. I hate this crap! I remember thinking, for the pellets hitting that frozen grass and pelting my aching back would still be on that front yard when the yellowlegs returned to Rockport, and on top of that hated sleet would be inches of packed and dirty snow, shoveled in places, stained with the splash of salt and dirt/grease that killed trees planted by a city forester. The lights of my city back five miles behind cast orange on the sleet clouds through driving frozen water, and the prairie wind blew with the freshness of a first storm of many. My jeans were stiff and white with the crusted salt of Rockport, and my mind was still sitting in the Mustang disappeared into the sands of Rockport Gulf. My key still fit my own front door, and inside I pulled off boots that seemed to have grown to my skin. I distinctly remember brushing the Gulf sand from my jeans into those boots. I always bring back sand from the Gulf, and when I get back into the laboratory I always look at that sand under a microscope. That sand is always full of the shells of amoebas.

Karen sat in her favorite place looking out through large glass doors onto a backyard with plantings, aglow in reflected neon from five miles away, accumulating then the white ice flecks that said yes, it was serious time for sleet now and that said no, it would not melt by morning. Nor by February. Perhaps not even by the time yellowlegs returned to Rockport. I remember thinking almost a year ago the same thoughts I always have when she sits in her favorite place: how well she fits the tall and slender purely Danish armed dining room chair; they might have been made for each other. The same thing could have been said for the wineglass she held hanging in two fingers, wrist resting on the knee of a crossed leg. I sat with my salt-caked jeans and socks still red, Oklahoma clay-stained, in a sister chair, and we looked at one another for a long time.

"I'm glad you're back."

"I'm glad to be back."

"Where have you been?"

"Texas. I followed the yellowlegs."

"They've been calling here for you."

"I guess I figured that would happen."

"Don't you care?"

"No."

"I guess I figured *that*; so I told them."

"Good girl."

Although she didn't ask, she knew what I'd been doing, the same thing I was doing when we met, the same thing I've been doing every day since we met, and now, after having followed the yellowlegs all last year, I would do until the minute I die.

"I've been studying some biology; teaching some biology."

She smiled and handed over her glass.

"Your vodka's in the same place it was when you left. Tonic's probably flat."

Kitchen colors moved through the liquid in her stemmed glass. Somewhere in the basement a television set was talking deep incoherence, and a minor child's argument drifted up the stairs. The tonic gave no sign of life. I did what I so often do at the end of such a day, such a week, such a time, filled the glass with ice and straight vodka. It's not so bad after the first sip.

"Going to tell me about it, or do I guess?"

"Doin' research and trying to teach a little biology, that's about it." But I started anyway, told of the days on the river, that first flock out by Grand Island, nightmares, our life savings, the bird, how it was banded, and how I got so close to it, but most of all how I spent all that time wondering who, just who in all this world, could have put that silver ankle bracelet on her. The television stopped doing whatever it was doing and there were steps on the stairs, an exclamation at the sight of boots, and the steps became running steps until there were small arms thrown around a father's neck, then another set of small arms and some small questions and small explanations. I was so glad a year ago to be exactly where I was, locked in those small arms, and the thoughts of a tomorrow with sleet did not please me then, for there would be intellectual and administrative sleet as well as nature's sleet, and all three would turn into packed ice glaciers of the upper midwest, but the white stuff on the ground would always melt before the yellowlegs returned to the Platte. The small arms came back in pajamas, and I sent them again down the hall with green carpet and told about buying a car, about a young man who might have been my own image of myself killing a sandpiper, the shotgun pounding through the Kansas air, and then of ponds and car trouble and jail and Texas and all those people I'd met and the thoughts I'd thought those lonely hours of research after that banded gray lady, and we talked late late into the night until again the front door slammed open, stumbled over boots, and slammed shut.

"Your father's home."

"Guess I figured that when I killed myself on his boots. Bring us anything?"

"I brought you some sand from Rockport. It's down in the boots; there's probably some here in my jeans if I shook 'em out. Find the most beautiful little amoeba skeletons in that Rockport sand; look at that sand under a microscope, see things so very few people on earth have ever seen, ever known about, much less thought about. Ever consider how that amoeba builds such a spiral architectural wonder? A single cell, with the genetic instructions for building one of the most beautiful and intricate structures known, a single cell, mind you, is an architect!"

"I'll tell all the kids at school; they'll storm the front door for your grubby boots!" I always smile at her smart talk. It's only her way of recognizing the truth and importance of something while at the same time recognizing the difficulty of conveying that truth and importance to others.

It was almost as if I'd never been gone. I was the same person, physically worn, perhaps, for the moment, but still the same person with the same thoughts and values as when I'd started this silly sabbatical, a stroll out along the Platte to see what I could see then, a stroll that ended with a trek alongside a yellow-shanked bird beside waters. I knew then that my responsibilities, if I were still employed, would begin again in the morning. My clothes would be the same clothes that were in my closet when I left on this research, and people would see me on the streets and assume I'd never been gone. But then I'd been gone many many times, and the animal subjects of my wanderings were only a few of the many places where I could easily become lost for days. We've been through all this for over twenty years now, Karen and I, this matter of being gone, and I suppose there are many things that people adjust to after more than twenty years. I guess she always survived my absence. I guess what always mystifies her is my ability to decide that I *require* whatever it is that takes me to these wildernesses. She also knows I'm about as much use to anyone when I'm on one of these mental migrations as I am when I'm physically absent. I suppose it's been lucky for us all that most of my sirens have been wild animals. I remember last fall, with the first sleet of winter rattling off storm windows, pouring another whole glass of vodka and taking it into the shower with me. Home. I was home. My migration with the yellowlegs was over; ended, finished; my sabbatical research complete. Those were my thoughts that night. I could not have been more naïve. I had forgotten that spring does come every year. It comes some time after winter. It brings back the sandpipers.

Her outline beneath the covers told me I was home from this migration, and her arm slung across my pillow told me she knew I was there; home. I could not remember so welcome a sense as that of my own place to sleep.

"You know your scoop shovel has the handle broken?" Her voice had the blurred edge of half sleep.

"I remembered that from last winter."

"But you followed the yellowlegs, and tomorrow you'll go out and shovel sleet with a broken-handled shovel knowing you have something no other human has." Her voice had the blurred edge of sleep and the smooth edge of total understanding.

"That's right."

"Dumb ass." I know her voice well; she had to be smiling in the dark.

Part III
SPRING

14 ⌒ A Visit to the Pleistocene

It was like taking an anesthetic.
Freezing was not so bad as people thought.
Jack London

I have rarely been wrong about winter; it's always my worst time. There is a stark beauty I sometimes watch in silence, but generally winter is the pits. Especially in Nebraska. I bought a new shovel. I added some antifreeze to my radiators. I had the studded snow tires put on the station wagon so Karen could drive it on the many terrible days she had deliveries to make. I closed and locked the door to the deck. She brought her plants inside. I read the paper and stacked firewood and went on a vodka diet. She started the fire and read the paper afterwards and had a glass of wine. I went to a very important committee meeting and so did she. I delivered myself to a laboratory/office with no windows and she delivered children to piano and dancing. I sat on the couch and watched her stalk the living room still dressed in nice clothes from a long day with the city's philanthropic old men, but she bent in her nice clothes to poke the fire and wondered how my mind was getting along in Argentina.

The clouds came from the northwest, and television weathergirls showed curving lines with sharp points sweeping down from places I'd never been, the Pacific Northwest and beyond to the Arctic. The curving lines and sharp points swept in out of the north with a roar and a darkened hiss and caught me on the way to a parking lot, blowing powder across whipping "Snow Emergency" signs. A tractor with a large canvas and plastic hood cleared sidewalks ahead. The world became dark very early, and the New Ice Age descended upon the Plains. Ice crystals blew against my skin, into my eyes, and in private moments I toyed with the idea that the yellowshanks was either in Argentina or dead. Argentina or dead. Either might be a viable alternative to a stroll on a sidewalk separated from Pleistocene glaciation by only a barbed-wire fence and final exams.

In my mind I became a mastodon. I pulled on jeans and boots, added a real leather belt with large brass eagle buckle, a shirt with snaps instead of buttons, heavy leather sheepskin coat, and forced my mastodon body out into the blizzard. The mastodon fought the gale blowing off the glacier, physically bending a shoulder into the slashing currents lashing out of crevices. The glacier towered above into the swirling haze and disappeared into the storm fury skies, but the mastodon made out vertical juttings through the screaming wind, so worked his way around those juttings of ice, looking, searching, for a haven to sit out an earth spasm sliding massive untold quadrillions of tons of polar wind down over a land that was supposed to break open for a yellowlegs in a hundred days. His haven leaked blowing snow, and the clay floor was slippery with melt. A stairwell made space symphony from the winds off the glacier, and he moved deeper into his haven. The mastodon awoke after his fifth cup of coffee made with triple glass distilled deionized water. It was not a glacier after all, only an empty football stadium, towering above the herds outside, and he was only a biology teacher at work for the day. But he concluded, staring at memorandums issued by memorandums issued by memorandums, that the Ice Age *had* returned and it was once again the Pleistocene up through the levels of his place of business. Argentina or dead; those were his alternatives to the Pleistocene that day.

He stalked his lair these days, while outside petrifying winds blew mortals against the cliffs, where they lifted eyes frozen in terminal pain to a shifting sky to see faces staring from windows half missing in the blowing snow. Thus the winter world went about its rounds. In his laboratory the mastodon manipulated the machinery and vocabulary of his trade. On other days he forced himself upon the blizzard that covered many states and fought the wind to another cave, this one large, cavernous, with sheer walls on all sides, upon which danced the images of electron micrographs, and in this cavern he arose among the young Neanderthals around the glowing embers of an unfettered time and passed along as if by secret the scientific discoveries of another culture. He was in a dream, and his chantings, songs of Solomon, incantations, tales of history and grand accomplishments, came back to him as mastodon sounds taken from the wind. Waw, waaannhw, whannnw, wa-a-a-a-w, waaa-a-a-a-aw, waw, waw, wa-a-a-annn-a-waaw . . . came the wisdom of the ages, at least as understood *this* Pleistocene. In the hierarchies above, well-groomed mastodons rested their ample haunches on high places and asked if he'd done his "waw-waw's" properly this year. The younger ones scattered over the cavern floor scratched his words on tablets, then brought their tablets, so he sat at great lengths talking to some, arguing with others, but often when they left muttering down the winding corridors of his laboratory mountain, a great sadness came over him. It *would* be spring; the yellowlegs *would* return; he *would* metamorphose back into a human being; the Pleistocene *would* end. This last one, he would assure: the Pleistocene *would* end, he would see to that.

When the younger ones left and went muttering down the corridors in half light, the sadness returned and remained. The young ones were the hope of this world. But as the objective scientist beast, he saw immense intellects walking away in the half light, intellects that some characteristic of this Pleistocene had forever sealed in the lamination of early decision. He was dumbfounded. She closed her tablet, smiled sweetly, wriggled into a woolen garment, retrieved hand-woven gloves for slender hands with a pewter ring, and left with a twist of her wrist. The click of her heels down the clay hall told him a set of brains humanity needed desperately had instead decided to become a dental hygienist. Her highschool counselor had told her it was a "good profession for women" and her parents, appalled at the cost of sending her away, had told her to *prepare for some kind of a job!* Her options were frozen when she came to the glacier. Her potential creative powers were lost to mankind in its direst time of need. The sulking mastodon returned slowly to a sinkful of dirty glassware and a bench top of machinery and chemicals. It *would* be spring. Flowers would bloom and birds would sing, and the cranes would return to the river. The yellowlegs would return to the plains and he would go welcome it. But the brain with the pewter ring would forever be a dental hygienist.

The intellectual glaciers advanced and retreated and in between came bursts of flourishing culture, and the mastodon came to view these bursts as historical events. Thinking back, he concluded that the glacial movements also influenced his own climatic changes, so that with each passing Ice Age the environment within him changed, became fertile for some planted ideas, less fertile for others. He began to look carefully at the origins of his own thoughts, as well as the origins of young Neanderthal thoughts. The world through which he walked had chosen him as "teacher," but most of what he did was talk, and most of what they did was write down what he'd said. So he remembered what he'd said, and he looked at what they'd written, and he then decided that the brain had not evolved to its present size and complexity because of the opposable thumb, nor war, nor bipedal locomotion. The brain had evolved in response to the difficulty of using language. The driving force of such co-evolution produced changes of such speed that in the hundreds of millenia later theoreticians would not be able to agree to which came first: language or brain. He never had difficulties with such theory. A biology teacher knows language came first. It forced evolution of the brain.

Words, parts of words, new words, meanings, implications, new implications and implications of combinations of implications, context, posture and body language to add or alter meanings or combinations of meanings, or meanings of combinations of implications, paralanguage, phraseology, languages within languages, dialects, languages with equal words but unequal grammars, expression abilities (enhanced and restricted), speech, talking, writing, formal and informal, good and bad, functional and non-functional, lucid and obscure, manipulative language, submissive phraseology and paralanguage, language that stirred the soul but never penetrated the brain, language that penetrated the brain *then* stirred the soul—the mastodon was in the language business. He hadn't known it was to be this way when he'd made the decision to become a scientist/teacher, but it so happened. So he stood in the Pleistocene cavern and told young ones to learn the words and grammar of biology, to learn those words and grammar until they became a functioning set of interworking parts living evolving changing in response to environmental alterations, seasons, contexts, with reactions and responses and uses and misuses, progression and regression, extending the abilities of the user, evolving into families and genera and orders of related languages, doing all the things a machine or yellowlegs could do over either quick time or evolutionary time. Language functions *also* in many ways like a machine?

Man makes machine to extend his powers; man is a machine of sorts. Yellowlegs is a machine, or at least functions like a machine: responding to energy sources, controlled, servomechanism'd, evolving as a diverging welter of rockets or other devices. Earth functions as a machine, interworking parts and established relationships, all capable of being broken as a piston rod or malconnected as a transmission linkage. Language is the driving force between evolution of the brain, then the two become synergistic, forcing each other into higher and faster repeated cycles of driving energy, each time spewing out thoughts, ideas for other devices, or of uses for existing ones. Could the higher algebra of machine evolution, the matrix and differential equations, transitive and commutative laws, non-linear function fields and topology come finally to explain and unify all of nature from the evolution of shorebirds to the evolution of political systems whose very existence in turn depend upon proper functioning of language device? The whole universe itself, is that also nothing more than an algebraic extension of the basic principles of a Ford Autocar? Yes, the mastodon concluded, yes, it is! Small wonder that he now placed such importance upon the teachings and attitudes of a grizzled Oklahoma auto mechanic who never belonged to no Country Club but could sure as hail make a Ford Autocar run right!

It was February now. A radio down the hall somewhere said the "high today was minus five degrees Fahrenheit," and my face burned from having been out in the wind. I looked out over the prairie into the new but light snow and wondered if my bird were alive somewhere down in the tropics, whether she was at this moment miles out over the Gulf with sharks and other big fish, whether she stood on the crystal beach at Yucatán, or whether she might even be one of the early ones at Rockport; already. I turned back into the inner recesses of my laboratory mountain and sought my lair. There were young ones waiting.

They smiled and hung their woolen garments on a chair and rattled their bracelets and asked a bunch of questions to which they already knew the answers. They were more intelligent and capable than men now cutting into the guts of other men in hospitals; they were more intelligent and capable than men now making decisions that turned two hundred and eighty million lives; they were more intelligent and capable than men in hundreds of thousands of challenging, exciting, testing, rewarding, roles in the human drama. They had no business letting those brains twiddle away until their children left home and their husbands chased secretaries and they looked into mirrors at forty-five-year-old wrinkles and thought what they might have done in the past. They had no business letting those brains twiddle away while populations exploded and all forms of energy became scarce and religious wars swept over the face of their planet and among all the confusion no one stopped to contemplate a human ecological niche lacking those pointed wings cutting the prairie air, that willowy call from the night above, and the wilderness in which to seek a future. I decided then and there I would not answer inane questions from superior students whose performances placed them in the upper reaches of ability but whose experiences to date said use that ability to prepare for what would become a menial job. I would fight that problem until the day I died! I was perfectly capable that day of deciding the Pleistocene would end then and there!

"Ever see a sandpiper?" I said to them as I poured boiling water from an Erlenmyer flask into a cracked cup with bitter instant coffee.

15 ⌒ Yellowlegs Starts Home

Art had embarked on an entrance into the
long tunnel where aesthetics met technology.

Norman Mailer

She left the *pampas* in the same manner she had left
Rockport: one day there, the next day not. There was one moment
totally unseen by any man when a four-ounce bird, now old by any
standard of migratory sandpipers, lifted high aspect wings, brought
them down in an arc, and in so doing so lifted itself the first two
inches of a several thousand mile flight. Summer was ending on the
pampas; summer was supposed to be starting in that land where I sat
shivering in my car, defroster running full blast. Across the
grassland she aimed her slender bill to the north and started home;
home to a place where she had first appeared as a downy chick and a
day later had run under the wing of a protective parent; home to a
place where she had built nest after nest and sent her own chicks,
like her in so many ways, out into a world that did not move over
much for a yellowlegs; home, her obligation to her genes fulfilled
for one more time provided she could negotiate two continents. The
Earth moved slowly around its star and the angle of light hitting
the *pampas* from that star changed. The rains that had filled miles of
low spots would stop. Someplace to the north she would appear one
day or one hour then be gone again. She might be noticed by
prowling jaguar or Indian.

161

The *pantanal* at summer's end was an untamed land within an untamed land, an island of islands far inland on an island continent joined to the Nearctic for only evolution's short breath of three million years. Dreary North American industrial society doctor, lawyer, po-lice chief, teacher, scientist, beggerman, thief, could thumb through a book and go to South America, a "sister" continent like no other sister, and see that the Neotropical with its glaciers and deserts, rain forests and cloud forests, mountains, coasts and monkeys, uncharted jungles and Tierra del Fuego, Andean spine and a bloody revolution, was an unfathomable place. A North American industrial thumbing through a book might well decide that of all places to visit, South America was *the* one, perhaps, if one spoke the language; or, more seriously, if one *knew where to start*! The familiar sameness of a world power nation viewed through smog-encrusted windows paled beside the rolling expanse, seemingly inaccessible to all but wild beast and bird, of The Neotropical Realm. Still, she had been there several times on her own wings and had none of these impressions. The *pantanal* was as much a part of her environment as the Platte River, a Kansas mudhole, or a Canadian nesting site. So she appeared one day, unwitnessed, unmarked, not noted in any human journal, upon the *pantanal* of southern Brazil, and landed somewhere in a trackless marsh located at a place on the map with no cities shown. The fourth grade, that is the time American elementary students study the geography of South America. An inquisitive fourth grader might hold a map of Brazil, look at the *pantanal* with no cities marked, and wonder what was there. On this day the answer could have been "yellowlegs."

By the time she arrived in Brazil three or four feet of summer rainfall had turned a hundred thousand square miles of yellowlegs habitat into trackless marsh broken only by island hummocks, tangled clusters of places where agouti ran, and the cries of jaguars. A human could have stood on the edge of one of those hummocks, listening to the movements of large cats behind him, listening to the sounds of large rodents being chased to their deaths by a whole spectrum of New World cats, and looked out over marsh and sandpipers as far as he could see. "Teeming" was the hackneyed word, the marshes of the *pantanal* were "teeming" with life, a carpet of shorebirds as far as one could see. But no human stopped or looked. She appeared somewhere in the marshes and disappeared somewhere in the marshes. Her departure was seen only by a jaguarundi, long otter cat body with mouth drawn back into bite smile. She might have been his breakfast another year. She would never see another jaguarundi in her life.

An older man and his wife sat on their veranda and talked of the night before and the morning ahead of them. The man was a writer of sorts and a naturalist of sorts, and for some years had found a niche on the *llanos* under the long protective wing of the Museum. It would end one day; he knew that. His profession was not one that promoted long stays and long roots, although it was one that permitted the fullness of experience that perhaps deep roots did not. He crammed his life with the richness of his world as it now existed, knowing he must taste the best and the worst of his habitat before he had to leave. He was not the kind of man who could go away taking only the daily troubles of a human population to talk about in the years that would follow. He savored it all: to the west the Andes climbed clothed in a succession of forest types to their heights; on the outskirts of town there remained virgin forests through which some men treaded softly but none dared to cut; a hundred miles to the south two of Earth's greatest rivers almost touched, but instead flowed their separate ways from isolated headwaters into the Orinoco and Amazon. The man stared out over the Orinoco basin. Open savannas were a few miles away and beyond that, the *llanos*. It was that time of year, and his manuscript lay unfinished on a desk back inside, back off the veranda where he sat with Colombian coffee in the morning, tasting both and thinking, perhaps, of mosquitoes. He looked over at his wife and she smiled back. His eyes said he was going to the field; they did not need to speak. When he returned later that evening they both knew another year had passed.

"The sandpipers are gathering," he said, and she knew then that he had been far out on the plains that day, out where the marshes lay and black water flowed into Venezuela. A village cat yowled outside the window and the man grimaced. He did not like cats;

they killed the birds that surrounded their home, although he did have to admit that in eastern Colombia there were probably enough birds to feed the local cats.

"They'll be gone soon," she replied, then wished she hadn't said it. The statement reinforced their isolation. It was sad to be away from a homeland. It was even more sad to not really want to return when surrounded by a beauty such as theirs. The sandpipers handled it every year, from beauty and the world's island-continent jewel headlong into the technological explosion of the Nearctic and back again. He spent some of his evening with the familiar conclusion that once again, the other species could do things he could not do: a sandpiper could pass from the *pampas* to the *pantanal* to Yucatán to Rockport to Kansas to Canada and back again and never experience the mental adjustments required of a human entering that long tunnel where aesthetics met technology. But then the sandpiper was a passive part of earth-machine, whereas human was an active participant in the running of that machine. The conflict beginning to manifest itself in his mind now hadbecome more and more frequent these recent months. He would have to return to his country sometime, just as did the sandpipers each year. He would welcome that return, but he would hate the leaving, and when he reached the Technological State, he would have arrived with those years on the *llanos* in his mind. He would have things no other human had. He would feel those things inside himself, and sometimes those things would give him comfort and sometimes they would give him pain. But they were his and he had them; they had become a part of him by now.

"The yellowlegs were out there in large numbers today."

Again she smiled. In a few weeks there would be no yellowlegs out on the *llanos* and he would be restless. One day, she thought, resigned to the eventuality, one day we will follow the yellowlegs home. Until then he would do the work of the Museum and wonder exactly what route, what daily stops, what close calls and experiences the sandpipers would take and had taken. They appeared then disappeared.

"I thought one of them was banded but couldn't really get close enough to tell for sure."

She raised her eyebrows at that. She had been around this man

long enough to understand the significance of seeing a banded
sandpiper.

Centuries had gone since the Mayans had been bypassed by
Spaniards seeking gold. Considered poor at the time, the Indians
were left alone for a while, during the time Conquistadors were
systematically laying to waste one of the most startling civilizations
ever to have existed. Having penetrated into Monteczuma's heart,
they then cast their eyes back toward the south, back toward
Yucatán, toward harsh scrub and jungle, dry, but crossed by rivers,
where exotic strangeness was symbolized best by hoards and clouds
of screaming birds no Spaniard had *ever* seen. European warrior
astride a European horse, both looking out over what would become
the *ruins* of Chichén-Itzá, had no way of knowing that the barn
swallows darting around them would almost five hundred years
later take some of the luster of unknown off the Yucatán Peninsula
for an American turista. Nor had warrior and horse any inkling of
the role this land had played in the movements of such small
animals. In 1523 there were no zoologists following sandpipers for
the sole reason of discovering where they went in the winter or
summer. The yellowlegs had passed over the carnage which would
later, almost five hundred years later, be known as a magnificent
tourist attraction, and those same yellowlegs had flown to what
would, almost five hundred years later, be known as Canada, and
those same yellowlegs had hatched chicks whose descendents
would, almost five hundred years later, be setting wings into the
mouth of a river, winding to a tired finish among the mangrove
lagoons and tidal flats of Río Champotón.
Her diet changed at the mouth of Río Champotón, and that
change produced some stress on the worm in her belly. Such worms
spent their time in the insect larvae of the *pampas* and in the
yellowlegs that wintered there, depending upon the birds for a
steady diet of free amino acids and sugar molecules, vitamins, fats,
salts of many kinds, and the worm had depended upon the bird to
not only supply these things but to regulate their concentrations
within the intestine. Thus the worm was bathed in a tightly
controlled soup; nutrient broth. Few animals could ever hope for a
place as warm and serene as the inside of a yellowlegs gut. The

worm placed no great stress on a healthy bird, and the bird placed no great stress on a healthy worm. Coiled back on itself in a constant state of intercourse the worm rode its feathered airliner out of the *pampas* across the *pantanal,* through a man's life on the *llanos,* and probably should have been told to fasten seat belts in preparation for landing. Out on the mudflats bordered by mangrove the shorebirds ran and she set her wings to join them. So she whiled away some warm days watching sport fishermen chug in from the laguna with tarpon to have pictures taken, and rested, and ate salt and brackish water animals that didn't quite taste right to a hyperfastidious tapeworm she was supporting, and made short flights, although she also became increasingly restless with the urgency, building every day, for a final dash to Canada. It was time to go soon, and in a lazy low trajectory she moved away from the congested sport fishing docks to the outskirts giving way to houses, and vacant lots, and finally mangrove and other brush where the poorer people lived. The small flocks dozed and stepped slowly in and out of the very shallow waters. The mixture of species was typical of a migration mudflat. There were yellowlegs on the flats not too far from the trees, and she set her wings in the familiar glide to join them, hearing distinctly their calls to her. She never saw the man with the ancient shotgun back in the mangroves.

"Tingüis chico!" His little boy crouched at his heels with pounding heart and tugged at the man's sleeve, pointing out over the mud, as the old man with Mayan profile raised a beaten shotgun with a single hammer and fired into the flock of yellowlegs. The recoil knocked him back but the boy was out on the flats with his bare feet before the smoke from the old shells cleared, picking up dead, wringing necks, chasing wounded. He chased a banded one but she was too fast and he turned rapidly, making random frantic little footprints in the mudflat, after others that he could catch, bleeding. Again the pellets had ripped through the mud and the sandpipers and again she was free and gone on high aspect wings with faired trailing edges. The twinge of hot pain would not have been necessary to frighten her, the sound of the shot would have been enough. She did not need the single lead pellet lodged deep within her breast muscles, blood clotting already as she fired those muscles and activated her flight programs surrounding that pellet,

torn track through her skin dragging her own feathers into her, lead already beginning to dissolve out into her body as she moved rapidly, high cruise, out over *Laguna de Terminos* on a landless flight for which she was not quite ready.

The woman's husband had died during the winter, but he had been old anyway and could no longer drive a car. He'd received most of his daily pleasure from coffee, laced slightly with brandy, a walk down the beach of Rockport, and his wife's tales of shopping and town. He'd had a great laugh over her trip north. Thought *she'd* died, he did, and worried for a while, but then read his books and laced his coffee some more and took his long naps in the afternoon and watched television for news of her and talked to the lady next door, a widowed girl in her fifties, and took his increasingly feeble walks on the beach, until one day not long thereafter she returned and appeared out on the driveway. Just like some of the birds of Rockport, he thought, and told her so, going and coming from places no one knows. He'd become ill, a few weeks after she returned, pneumonia among some other things, and passed away shortly after Christmas. She was very sad for him, but the sadness soon gave way to other, better feelings, feelings of which he would have been proud had he still been alive, feelings which set her apart from so many of the other girls whose husbands had gone.

"He had a good long life, old bugger," she said one day, "gave lots and took lots. Got nothing to be ashamed of, no terrible bad debts, and he's probably in heaven now where he belongs. When you can't drive a car any longer or get around much, and you've had your kids and your women and put away your brandy and worked your soul to the bone and whiled away your years at the end, then what's left?"

The girl in her fifties from next door agreed. Or at least appeared to agree; she nodded her head and said nothing. It was that time of year in Rockport. The older woman took her binoculars and went to the beach not too far from where a police wrecker had towed a wretched white Ford Mustang with black markings out of the surf and sent the owner a fine, and a bill for towing charges, and a letter telling him not to ever cross the city limits of Rockport again. The sandpipers were beginning to gather once more. The search for the first yellowlegs now gave her more pleasure than she'd ever known in the last few months. She was glad Christmas in Rockport was over; she was glad spring in Rockport was here. She looked out over the Gulf of Mexico, saw the gulls turning, and thought she saw a flock of shorebirds moving purposefully in the faded light, but she couldn't tell for sure. She went home and watched television but fell asleep during Carson. She awakened on the couch late at night and the lights were still on.

If a shorebird had emotions, human emotions, the lights of Rockport, beginning to appear now in the dusk, would have been the most welcome of sights. Far out over the Gulf she had seen them, and although she could not detect the driving forces within her, there was some force that pulled her again and again to familiar places. The lights came closer with each contraction of pained muscles on the right side, and she was very tired at this time. She had no memory of emotional or intellectual states, so she could not remember whether she had ever been this tired at the end of a Yucatán-to-Texas jaunt, but she was weakened and exhausted when her feet finally touched the shoreline of Rockport. The lead pellet still dissolved and her metabolic machinery shifted its equilibrium slightly with every atom of lead that entered her bloodstream. A festering scar ran up through her flight muscles where the pellet had entered, and as the small surf washed up around her ankles, she looked out into the gloom and stared for what must have been a long time at a gray and white cat working its way around the pilings. Anyone attempting a flight across the Gulf of Mexico would be relieved at landfall. It might not matter immediately that landfall was the first step upon a shore that off in the distance contained industries that dumped thousands of *new* kinds of compounds into water supplies every year, that spread oil upon mud that looked from the air like water, that raised towers for the projection of energy, towers that snapped the necks of warblers and robins alike, that placed guns in the hands of little boys at early ages, that kept cats for the enjoyment of the cold predatory approaches of those animals, that killed cats for the same behavior, that drained prairie wetlands, that shot random birds when ducks or doves weren't flying, that built dams across rivers with broken rock beds beneath, that drove used cars and filled the air with more fumes and chemicals, and that in the final analysis would always be modified to support as a first, and usually only, priority a species other than the yellowlegs.

The worm in her gut should have been sick by now, malnourished by northern hemisphere food. Instead it writhed and twisted and maintained its place with uncommon vigor. The lead shot had indirectly changed its home slightly, but that slight change in the metabolism of a female lesser yellowlegs allowed a tapeworm that ate only molecules to survive, and prosper, knot in belly, grinding taking knot twisting in belly, when instead it should be dying of starvation or old age. The worm and the sandpiper still had to make it to the airport a thousand miles north if they were to watch the private jets screaming in to check out spring football practice.

16 ᴄ On the River Again

. . . and then, with a few long, running
strides takes to his wings, at the same time
sounding his wild and defiant cry.
George Gladden

There is an event that happens in this country every year.
That event heralds the return of spring; it's called arrival of the
sandhill cranes. There are those who say this "arrival" is an un-
natural phenomenon, occurring only in recent years, now that the
Platte has been manipulated, altered, domesticated, and only a
short stretch remains wild. There are those who say this fifty-mile
stretch of river upon which the cranes move in spring is a
"concentration" that did not exist in ancient times. In ancient
times, it is said, cranes used the whole river on their trips north,
but now they stay along a stretch about fifty miles long. During the
day, the cranes don't stay much right *on* the river; mainly they're
out along the fields of corn and milo stubble, dancing away. For
some reason they don't stop on our river in the fall. Too much of a
hurry to get on down south, I suppose, so cranes on the Platte is a
spring event.

The Pleistocene glaciation also begins to melt some time in
March. It is not really warm in March, or green, but there are days
scattered in March when Winter inhales, gathering strength for
increasingly difficult and weak forays from its January home, and on

170

these days the shade is jerked from a window that looks out over summer. One can sense the warm coming, and a light jacket is worn, the sun shines, the wind is calm, and cars begin to gather outside garden shops. Old men, used to the latitude, dig in their yards. Light comes finally to the plains about the twentieth of March. I know the morning well—that is my private time for spiritual communications with Joseph Mallord William Turner—and by the twentieth of March I have seen the year's mornings and can tell you that most of them have been dark. Light comes to the plains on the twentieth, however, and creeps over the tops of neighbors' houses, runs quickly through back yards and up alleys, splatters on large suburban buildings, hospitals, water towers, martin houses, Ford Agency signs, runs along power lines into town, kicks stones along Main Street, graces railroad tracks with a touch of sparkle then ducks into the inner city. With the light comes the cranes. Six months ago it was the twentieth of March, a typical day out on the prairies, about like I've just described, nothing magical or mystical about the twentieth of March, just a typical day out on the prairies. Except that on that typical day out on the prairies the cranes called and I heard.

It's a hundred and twenty miles from here to Kearney, that town in the middle of crane country, so you must know that it is only pure fantasy for me to say I heard the cranes calling. But there are those of you who believe in the unbelievable, the communications across time, in media not all know exist, the visions not all can have, in colors not all can see, at frequencies not all can hear. There are those of you, I know, for I have met and talked with you, who believe mankind is headed for a destiny in which our very molecules will communicate through electromagnetic waves with the DNA Mother in the Core of the Galaxy. There are those of you, I know for I have talked with you, who have sat in the curtained back room of a house down in the south part of this town and listened while an old old woman spoke with your relatives from the past. There are those of you, I know for I have been in your presence, who can raise a book from the table with your thoughts, who can read my mind and tell me my ideas in a foreign language not of this planet. So I know that there are at least some of you who will believe me when I say that about six months ago, on a typical day out on the prairies, the cranes called and I heard.

I stood at a mailbox and dropped in an envelope addressed to the "Internal Revenue Service, Ogden, Utah," but there came across the prairie the call of the cranes, and I stood for a long time at that mailbox, searching a prairie sky, before deciding it was only a truck, or a train, or the tornado horn being tested up on some school. I turned my head to better catch the sound of those wings, standing off in some bay of a filling station, and listened for those wings a great long time before deciding it was only the sound of an air wrench biting on the lugs that held my studded snow tires so firmly in place against the Pleistocene. You must know that by the end of the Pleistocene a man who makes his way through this world as a studier of animals is ready, nay, *vulnerable,* to those communications that call a heart back to the river. I had thought many times through the winter of the yellowlegs, but somehow the Pleistocene has a way of insulating your mind against the reality of wilderness. When it's dark when you get up, dark when you go to work, and dark when you get home, and through all those travels the blue of packed snow fills your world, then it's hard to remember that you actually did some research into the natural history of a wild thing. Oh, the values are still there, the deeper alterations of being, and those values influence your daily life, but the physical reality of research into the natural history of *Tringa flavipes* has a way of fading into the past during the Pleistocene. But on that typical March day out on the prairies when the cranes call, and you can hear them in the sounds that signify your city, then you know it's time to go again, back to the river.

There was a fog over the Platte before daybreak, and I sat on the fender of my ancient, oh so ancient, Mercury, beneath cottonwoods along a gravel road. To the south, out through the mist, was a field of corn stubble from last fall, and across that field another line of trees, still brown in the distance, but with the faintest cast of green; and it was cold. My jeans were worn from the Pleistocene, and my field jacket collar was turned up against the wet chill of a stirring winter's end prairie. Intermittent wind whistled once in the swelling branches above, then made no more sound for a while. A cardinal pierced the morning unseen from what must have been a farmstead down the road behind the fog and half light. Small sparrows flittered tiny shadows through the yellow cottonwood leaves and whitened fallen cottonwood branches of last year, piled down in the bar ditch. There was cracked soil beneath those fallen branches, and in a few weeks spring rains would flood that puddle and there would once again be mosquitoes. It was all very still, except for the cardinal, that early in the morning, but there came from who knows how far into the mist a sense, maybe only a feel that there would be a sense, of a call.

You must accept that there are ways of passing vibrations between entities, ways that have yet to be described by any scientist, and not only that, you must accept that I am vulnerable to some of those ways. Those forces jiggle molecules within key cells, and six months ago I could not but feel those forces. I strained to hear the sound again, and again came a *sense* of a call from out in the fog, an insistent call, a wild call, and I remember thinking it was only the cold that sent a shiver of wildness through these forty-year-old bones. I turned first the eyes, then ears, into the mist, straining for the connection, the communication, seeking needing asking for the sound that came again and again, and again and again, more strongly then, *the* call, the chorus of calls, the guttural grating resonant calls, in harmony, in synchrony, over and over, heralding, trumpeting guttural and resonant, announcing, stronger and stronger and stronger, the wildest sound ever to be heard out on a river, a sound that wrenched the heart in its socket and turned it to the primeval against its will, a sound out of the prehistoric, a sound of total wilderness and insignificance of human being species ill-equipped indeed for life in the *real* wilderness. The sound came rolling through the morning, surrounding, dinning and pounding from every direction, from back into ages when only savages lived, stronger, chorus, guttural, stronger stronger louder *louder* LOUDER UNTIL AT TREE HEIGHT CAME WAVE UPON WAVE OF GLIDING WINGS SET TAKE POSSESSION OF THE AIR AND THE MIND THOUSANDS AND THOUSANDS UPON THOUSANDS OF GRAY ONES ANNOUNCING TO

THE WIND THAT THE CRANES HAD RETURNED TO THE RIVER.

They settled into fields, some falling in the most awkward of postures from high out of the mist lifting with the first heat of a sun that had broken through a tree line far to the east. And as far as any human could see as the mist moved higher and higher into vapor, there were cranes.

You must know that out on the river with cranes, in the spring upon the Platte in Nebraska, there also returns your feeling that all things are possible. Not only that, there returns the feeling that all things are reasonable, all actions, all ambitions and good ideas, and something has migrated back north with the sandhill cranes. "It's all right to be a biologist after all," you hear yourself saying, "this is my place and these are the things with which I belong." There is a flood and a rush of spring in those thoughts. There is a freedom, a desire, of renewal that can only come back in the spring, rushing into your frozen rituals of the Nebraska Winter in ways that you suddenly realize you've wanted for so many bleak months of darkened cold. I don't know how those feelings and realizations come to the surface in others, but for a biologist, it's sheer orneriness. There was only one thing left to do that day when the cranes returned to the river, and you know without me saying what that one thing was, six months ago.

It doesn't rain much in Nebraska in March, no, most of the rain comes later. But it rains in Kansas in March, and the water accumulates in standing puddles, sometimes several acres in size, off in the corners of some winter wheat field. The sunflowers are dead and brown in March, around those rain puddles, but in March you can see teal out in those puddles, and killdeer along the edges, but most of all you can see real sandpipers. Their long wings cut the prairie air and their legs trail total grace, and they sometimes twist and turn, calling their soft and insistent calls, as they set gliding into that rain puddle off in the corner of some field. And you must know that when you're sitting on that car fender in March, having been called to the river by the wildest sound of all nature, and you know it's rained in Kansas, and it's spring and that flood of freedom and desire for renewal has been released, and that those feelings will come to the surface in a biologist as sheer orneriness, then there's only one thing to do. You punch a cassette into your ancient Mercury's tape player, with Bill Monroe and the wildest call of the five string banjo, turn it up full blast volume, and aim that second-hand piece of junk out hurtling across the prairies south into Kansas to see if you can find a yellowlegs.

17 ⌒ Yellowlegs on the River

. . . in checking well drillings . . .
there will be found species whose ranges
are long . . .

J. A. Cushman

*P*atrolman Gates, State Highway Patrolman Gates, to be exact, was proud of his vehicle as he stood on the interstate bridge near the south bank of a half-mile-wide braided prairie river. His boots were polished, even the tops, perhaps especially the tops beneath tan gabardine pants, the latter with razor creases. Patrolman Dodge, State Highway Patrolman Dodge, to be exact, could never for the life of him figure out how Gates was able to keep those pants creased and so wrinkle free. They both ran the same miles in their Ford Modified LTD, sat beside one another on the same seat, stopped beside the same minor repairs out in the blowing wind and hurtling semis of state and Federal highways. Dodge always had wrinkles, or at least some. Gates was always razor sharp and immaculate. These were the problems on Patrolman Dodge's mind today. Gates, on the other hand, had no problems today, other than the one immediately at hand, so he thought of his Ford, big supercharged engine, oversized steel-belted radials, packed with electronic gear, a *machine* worthy of the name, and he thought a little bit about poor Dodge, always concerned about his appearance. So he watched Dodge for a while, directing traffic out on the bridge, and thought maybe if a wrinkled uniform could hold a man back in the Patrol, then Dodge would probably be held back, regardless of how good he was, and others would get their promotions, regardless of how bad they were, if their pants were creased. Ain't that hell! thought the older Gates, and nodded at the station wagon with children at the windows, slowed now, waiting for directions, family wide-eyed, trying to see up ahead, father driving, trying to see and still not have a minor accident of his own. Station wagon tires crunched glass out on the bridge a few yards, and Gates followed the car with his eyes. It passed slowly and safely over two hundred yards of screaming black parallel gouges in the asphalt. Gates had thought about closing off this whole section of the highway, sending these families around through town, but the wind was blowing strongly and whatever fumes there were were blowing off the bridge. Luckily for the cleanup crews, most of that tank truck's load of chemicals had spilled off the bridge and was washing down the river. Gates was exceedingly relieved he did not also have a fire on his hands; that could have been a douzy. The tanker was splattered and twisted and hanging partly over the bridge railing, and the driver was also splattered and twisted and hanging partly over the bridge railing. A lot of people drove very carefully the next few miles after crossing Gates' bridge.

Fertilizers to feed a gluttonous metropolitan area and starving Third World nation, records with the London Symphony, tapes with Marshall Tucker, plastics of all kinds and shapes and colors, insecticides, additives for your car, drugs for your body, complicated molecular wastes, specially synthesized research chemicals and chemicals for chemical warefare, shampoo bottles, preservatives, paints, cloth and clothes, "rubber," virtually all of nature in texture, tensile strength, rigidity, plasticity and color, virtually all, was reproduced by the petrochemical industry or some offshoot of it. Neither Gates nor Dodge thought much about the petrochemical industry except at times like this. They never wondered much about what those chemicals were, what they would eventually end up being, but only whether they were dangerous to humans in the immediate vicinity and whether they were likely to explode. Neither one paid much attention to the river bed, now with what seemed like a half-acre swatch of black/dark brown seeping into the sand and casting a rainbow surface over moving, but smooth, waters. Already nature was sorting through this mess and it was only an hour old. Many species died, and of those, some would not return to the river for many years, maybe a generation. Many species ate the stuff in one way or another, and of those many had the metabolic machinery to store it, or convert it, into some un-natural molecule. Many species' populations would decline sharply for many miles down river, but others, relieved of the competition, would flourish. The disruptions would fade away after several miles, be diluted. Almost in the same manner as downstream from a dam, the river *would* return. There would also be, as below a dam, miles of river that looked like a river but were not: something missing, something added, something altered, and so some question about this river's ability to serve as an avenue to some creature's future. No flying sandpiper could ever detect the chemicals in an insect's body, or a subtle film of chemical on sand and waters that looked wild. Gates had read the labels on the truck before he'd even looked at the driver, and he'd radioed in to discover the tank truck would probably not explode and that the fumes would probably not kill people as long as the mass was not down in some windless hollow in the hills. The stuff did not smell all that great, and it made a strange stain on the bridge paving. He tried not to get it even on the soles of his polished boots.

Sandpiper season finds them stuck away in the most common and unexpected of places as well as the most uncommon and expected places. Broad sandy expanses of prairie rivers in spring always come with breeding pairs of killdeers. They run a ways, complain, then run some more, in slightly different directions, then complain some more, then take to the air with a flutter of complaints and punctuate their driving wing beats with the unique calls from which they get their names. The smaller peeps skitter and nervously dissect the places where the river has moved during the night, leaving exposed mud bars and driftwood. The large avocets and stilts stalk the sand but are not comfortable on the river, frighten easily, and move off to larger marshes a few miles away.

Yellowlegs out of the air from Yucatán sets wings and banks parallel to the meandering channel before settling well away from last year's cottonwoods, grown large enough to hide a raccoon or feral cat but not large enough to withstand spring floods a few weeks away. Yellowlegs out of the air from Yucatán is weary and in pain and does not run but walks with measured steps and stiffened muscles before moving out into the water, water touching her breast feathers now, wingtips and tailtips dipping into the oily surface film, film from Gates' and Dodge's truck miles upstream, and begins to feed the knot in her belly with larvae. The larvae are special this year: they are flavored with a chemical never intended to be metabolized by any cell anywhere. The flavoring soaked into whatever fat she had left, and into her flight muscles, and into the tapeworm in her gut, and stayed there, accumulating in all those places as she fed that day and the next, getting less and less able to move her wings with every passing hour. The chemicals stuck to her feathers and would not wash out. Nor did she have the enzymatic equipment to dispose of the molecules in her tissues. Just as there are things a sandpiper can do that no human can do, there are things the petrochemical industry can do that no sandpiper can do. Traffic upstream across the interstate bridge saw those black screaming gouges and knew something dreadful had happened. That's about as far as their concerns went. No biologist was there to tell them stories of sandpipers and to tell them that something dreadful had indeed happened.

The total intricacy of the bird as a working device now began to manifest itself. Somewhere in the depth of cells, bathed in a nutrient broth of cytoplasmic soup, lay the heart of life as manifest in *Tringa flavipes*. Strands of molecules, units, bases, sugars, six-membered rings, phosphates, matched, coiled, twisted, provided with mechanisms for covering and uncovering portions, were there in the depths of each cell in the form of a *Tringa flavipes* nucleus. The "genetic code": human scientists had deciphered it, they said, and assigned letters to molecules. They had begun dissecting its language, taking apart the control mechanisms of bacteria, so that although they may not have been able to identify a yellowlegs out on the river, they nevertheless were convinced the workings of a bacterial cell were as generally similar to those of yellowlegs as to any living thing. A strand of molecules linked by sugars and phosphates, with each molecule given an English letter, thus produced a diagram of a string of English letters. To the molecular chemist the string of English letters would spell *Tringa flavipes* as well as the *t*s and *p*s of a Latin name.

A program was that string of molecular letters, a program of information, a necklace of genes, first read by a fertilized egg within a mottled shell tucked away short years ago in the wild places of Keewatin. With the readings had come the stirrings of boiling cytoplasms and yolks. For long since the dawn of spoken communication, the earliest times of history, it has been known by all men that readings caused stirrings. Tucked away within a mottled shell beneath a female yellowlegs, heart pounding with possession, emotional possession of a *NEST* with *HER EGGS,* that first set of stirrings had produced two cells from one. A sandpiper in romantic and vulnerable innocence had done something no raging scientific establishment could do: construct a cell. Years later there would still be legions daily engaged in the blows of a knockdowndragout fight with the mysteries of cell division, the construction of cells. The scientists' labor also stemmed from emotion: the control of uncontrolled cell division was the goal; the understanding of malignancies. It remained to be determined whether a greater uncontrolled malignancy would also eventually kill the Ultimate Machine Earth Planet. Perhaps a value system that said it was "good" to be mesmerized by a study of uncontrolled cell division, but not "modern" to wonder why a yellowlegs would choose this river today with its poisoned insects, perhaps that value system was a malignancy worthy of study. Devastating tumors might well have had humbler beginnings. Devastating tumors might also have been as misdiagnosed until they had grown too far. Devastating tumors might also have been as ignored on purpose, thinking that prayers and a will to live might provide the psychosomatic cure for a terminal disease, not realizing that only the converse could be true.

So she stayed on the sand while the mess upstream was cleaned, and traffic resumed its flow hidden from her. She stayed for another day and another. Her hormonal regulatory mechanisms urged her northward, pulling, yanking at times, north, go north, sandpiper, go north, don't tarry along the way, go north, go north . . . and return to the spot where a falcon ripped into your adolescent trying wings for a trip to those places you've been: to Rockport, to a flat in

Yucatán, to the braided prairie rivers, to the flooded fields of Kansas stubble. Go north, sandpiper, for north is your place; do not wait for stray housecat, boy with gun, go north to meet your mate for this year. But the lead shot in her breast told her to stay, and the pain and the chemicals, the tapeworm, a South American tapeworm in a strange land surviving on molecular adjustments of a yellowlegs' metabolism—all told her to stay, stay, yellowlegs, stay and feed, stay where it's warm. It was a luring message; a message of death. To stay on the river for this creature at this time of the year would be the end. Sandpipers did not belong here soon. In the end, that message of death had to be subdued, ignored, overridden. She lifted wings with the tips soiled by a film of chemicals and heavy. She lifted wings with the energy from chemical reactions permanently adjusted to a lower level than that of unshot members of her own species, some far to the north by now, calling her, it might almost seem, wanting her and calling her but unable to help. She raised her wings and flew north; north to meet a scientist.

She had no idea of how long it might have been when the calls reached her, or how long she had moved those wings nor how far they had carried her. She saw the land beneath her and the marshes and mudholes scattered over that land. They all passed below as they had before on this route until the calls drifted up into the earthy air above a plowed field with small stretches of standing water, left for days now after a prairie storm. *"Pill-e-wee . . . pill-e-wee,"* they came, soft from below, the same haunting sound of a call given in a prairie tavern by an old man, a prairie tavern with a clear place on the window through which a shaft of light had fallen on a yellowshanks feather held by a smoky old man. Again she set her wings into the long curve glide, twisting down, until she saw the small flock that had called her home. They were beautiful and healthy, and there were males and they were young. These things were always noticed this time of year. Only an ornithologist, or another who had reason to know, would have looked from a two-lane highway into a field with standing water, knowing there would be something to be seen. She was very weak now, especially compared to the others, but had she the analytical workings of a human, she would have felt the strength of companionship that would have told her to fly north, make her best effort to fly north to the end of spring and the beginning of a new generation of yellowlegs. It was never to be.

Tomorrow.

Tomorrow would be the day she would meet this man who had followed her to land's end and could not then do the things she could do.

18 ⌒ In a Kansas Kitchen

With a voice soft and trembling
she'd sing her song to cowboy . . .
The Oak Ridge Boys

*I*t is all the same; I've done it a million times, this turning south into Quivera, the place the white man has come to call Kansas and a million times have smelled the ground, the sunflowers, the cattle and oil, the hot spring sun leaching these smells from a reserved land and opening the minds of a people I have always loved in a place I've always had good luck. I have traveled Kansas a million times; in winter, glazed; in summer, asphalt soft from the heat and combine crews suffering in thick yellow dust. It looked good this year, the still-green wheat, and I wondered how much of it would be pounded into the ground by hail a day before it was due to be harvested. The almost-reached time and place, that had to be the ultimate frustration for these people, to bring along that crop for all those months, to contract with the combine company, then to have it all cut short by the vagaries of a prairie storm.

Barbed wire. I always watch barbed wire from the highways. Funny how I'm always able to see barbed wire and funny how it always affects me. I'm almost always depressed by barbed wire. Not that it represents a hindrance, or restriction, but more something that a person does then leaves but then is obligated to, while at the same time its arrangements reveal owners' personalities in a way no neighborhood gossip could. My eyes darted to the fields and back to the road beneath my wheels, but there was no traffic, only a few pickups stretched out miles and miles apart, so I searched the fields until a few hundred feet off the highway I saw the yellowlegs standing and feeding in temporary water. I began searching for a farmstead to ask permission to crawl through the mud for a closer look, just to see, mind you, just to perhaps see, if one had a silver ankle bracelet that had been to another part of the world?

I read the barbed wire and knew what to expect. I was not surprised as I turned into the pink gravel driveway, still wet with last night's rain, and was met by several dogs. The place crawled with cats, and my skin crawled in harmony with their movements around unpainted sheds. Early sparrows moved in short purposeful spurts to lice-filled holes in those buildings, holes bursting with bales of grass woven by those sparrows into places only a sparrow could love. I never liked these kinds of places. I don't think a person should have to ask permission just to look at a sandpiper!

One never knows the financial situation of these people, although they always cry out hard times. I have seen them dirt poor and living dirt poor; I have seen them filthy rich and living dirt poor; and I have stood on a gravel driveway with some guy straight from the bowels of the earth and had that man tell me his daughter was in the Juilliard School of Music. One always expects a tractor parked somewhere, but one is never quite prepared for the cost of a new tractor. These people bear that cost, and my people hear about it and smile, for they cannot truly believe what these people bear for their freedom. As I unbuckled a seat belt my eyes took in the old tractor, rusted green, standing off between unpainted buildings near a barbed-wire gate, and the new tractor, fresh green, with its nose in one of those buildings and its high haunches filling the doors of a shed never intended to hold a *modern* tractor. The old tractor would still start; something about its posture told me that. This place could easily belong to a Master Mechanic of the land, one who would always keep the place running with the most simple tools of his trade, one who would always make it perform when others could not. The sparrows gave their insistent rolling chirps over and over again. Cats prowled and slinked, one recent litter hanging together. Some shovels and hand garden tools stood at the back door. I knocked. One always goes to the back door out here. The front door is always hidden by shrubbery.

I banged again, this time harder, and heard stirring inside. Heavy boots stepped on sheet linoleum back behind a torn screen and opaque glass. These people never speak when they arrive at the back door, only wait, politely asking with their eyes what it is the stranger could want, expecting requests for permission to hunt, to fish, directions somewhere, to report an accident, ask where one could buy eggs, fresh country eggs—those were the kinds of questions asked by uncomfortable visitors at back farm doors out of cars with city license numbers, and each of these questions had a season.

None of these questions was in season six months ago. My insides pounded and the world existed nowhere except on these crooked concrete steps. The body was large but did not fill the entire door; the face and hands had a familiar look, I could not figure it out; and my tongue fought for the right words as it always does these times, mangy tom rubbing my legs, wiping its back back and forth on my shin, repulsive, and other skittering beneath the house where I knew they were screwing themselves into more and more litters that would never see a vaccination against anything. Back behind the man I could see home canned things lining a back porch set of shelves.

"Like to ask permission, permission to cross the barbed wire back down the highway about a mile and take a look at those sandpipers around the big puddle. Can you tell me who owns that stretch back the other side of the trees?"

"Looking for sandpipers?"

"Big rain puddle back down the road almost a mile, just the other side of where that creek crosses." I pointed in the morning sunshine to a treeline gray brown with faint haze of first green. "Sandpipers are gathering around that big puddle. Can you tell me who I need to see to get permission to simply look at those birds?"

"Birdwatcher?"

"No guns; I have no guns, only binoculars."

"Could see you didn't have no gun." The man grinned. "That's our property; probably all right to go in there. Cattle's off in the south pasture. If it hadn't rained, you could probably get in there through the south pasture." The man pointed off towards a cattle gate. "Never get through there in *that* car."

"I'll walk; I'd rather walk."

"After sandpipers, you say?"

"Sandpipers. I'm from the university and we have a research project on these sandpipers." I lied with a perfectly straight face in a language I thought any lay person should be able to understand. "We're studying their movements and migrations; just need really to confirm the species out around that puddle for our records this time of year." Records indeed! I had need of the sight of that bird in a way no other living person could be told!

"Not nearly so many of those wild animals around here these days," said the face in the doorway. "Used to you could always see those little lizards runnin' from the tractor, big flocks of those sandpipers. Now mostly just sparrows and these cats." He pushed one aside as it tried to slip into the house. Back behind him a woman and two boys were moving in the kitchen. I was patient as could be, straining to get on with it, waiting for the simple way to excuse myself from a place I felt really didn't want me around!

"Thank you, I'll just park up by the road and walk in. It can't be too far; I could see them from the highway." I could see the yellowlegs from the highway! I could see the yellowlegs from the highway! They're *there!* They're *back!* I could see them from the highway!

"Ever need any specimens of those things?"

It was my own turn to be suspicious, and I looked carefully at the man for what seemed like a long time.

"I don't need any today."

"Just wonderin'," said the man, "if you ever use any specimens of those little sandpipers. Got one inside here; cats brought it in, probably from that rain pond. Be happy to give it to you. Kids think they can keep it alive, been givin' it some bread, but it don't seem to want to eat much."

"I would be interested in seeing it." I spoke with the calmness that only a scientist faking ignorance can muster. "Yes, it would be interesting to see exactly what kind it was." I was dizzy for a moment, out on the concrete steps.

186

"Come on in. Kids got it here in a box, keep it away from the cats. Like I said, it don't seem to want to eat much."

I nodded politely to the wife, who smiled back a leathery smile, and spoke familiarly to the boys, who tumbled over one another to assure me they had not shot the banded lesser yellowlegs standing on yesterday's newspapers in the bottom of a cardboard box. I stood staring down at her, just staring, staring for a long time, not reaching, not touching, just looking at the migratory machine within easy hand's grasp, reviewing all the travels and troubles and thoughts of the last year, wondering where to go from here and what to do from here and what would eventually become of me and all this business of chasing sandpipers and trying to do what a biologist is supposed to do: teach the world the value of things that work like yellowlegs, teach the people of the world they are an integral part of the place they live, not its only part. The bird moved and I reached for it. Even in pain and weakness it moved away from the hand, into another corner, and tried its wings, but they would not work and I knew it. I moved more quickly and grasped it by the back with my left hand, long neck and shapely head poking out through the index and middle fingers, legs treading air, long yellow legs treading air, but that should have been treading the mud marshes of some northern plains instead of newspapers in a steamy Kansas kitchen full of cats and little boys that probably also owned guns.

"This is a very interesting bird," I said, watching from the corner of my eye the mother putting the last sandwiches in a bag for each of the boys. The school bus will be here anytime, I thought, I must hurry, I must hurry but not hurry, I must take these people totally by surprise and not let them get away onto a tractor or school bus!

"Yes, this is a very interesting bird," I repeated, spreading the wing, the boys now leaning on the table with their elbows. "It probably flew all the way from South America within the last few weeks and probably was on its way to Canada."

"My friend shot one of them things one time."

"I bet he did," I replied, but went on with the tale. I stood beside the kitchen table and went on with the tale, the wildest tale of migration, of nesting in the northern wilderness, of long flights, of South America and places where jaguars lurked. I held the bird gently and could feel its weakened condition but explained the anatomy, spread the wing feathers and told their functions, showed the skin of the legs, the joints, told what the bones looked like underneath and within the animal machine, but finally, and above all, told a tale of values and appreciation, blind value and blind appreciation in the absence of practical importance of detailed knowledge, in the end a tale of the romantic that assumed this single bird was an essential part of a complicated second-hand machine called Earth. In the end, I told a tale a Master Mechanic would have told, of parts included with the right amount of élan, the right amount of feel, that would always make an Ultimate Machine go, even when one might not know exactly what that part was *for*. The bird became the symbol of all that is unknown and unappreciated, of all that must be explained and justified in practical and economic terms to warring nations and strapped state legislatures alike but cannot be so explained, so then suffers death, death as an idea, and I launched into my lessons on the deaths of ideas, of the dangers of always having to explain and justify to governments and rulers and administrators, when in fact the requirements should be that those governments and their pawns should have to explain to *us* just *why* they did not put proper romantic value on so fine a machine as Earth, so fine a machine as Yellowlegs, machines a Master Mechanic would have understood without really understanding.

They watched in silence as I finished in silence, the bird struggling.

"It can't fly," said one of the boys, "cat got it. We took it out in the yard and threw it up a few times, but it can't fly."

"I know."

"What are you going to do with it, mister?"

"I don't know; I really don't know."

I stared at the animal in my hand, and my eyes ran a mental paintbrush over the patterns of the feathers. The bird struggled more weakly then, as I spread the wings. I always spread the wings whenever I handle any bird. I could not bring myself to look at the band, the worn aluminum and dirty silver anklet that flopped loosely up and down on the long yellow leg.

"Ought to report that band number, shouldn't we?" The mother had spoken at last.

"I will report the band number."

"Won't get in any kind of trouble, will we, for having that bird?"

"It's all an accident; there is nothing you can do; I will report that."

I ran the long flight feathers through my fingers, and they did not feel quite right. The texture was wrong, and I rubbed my fingers together and thought I felt a film of some kind. It was a film, I was sure then, and I raised the wing to smell, placing the feathers against my nostrils, but the bird turned its head and laid a long cool bill against my cheek, trembling slightly, and I could feel the bill and small forehead against my unshaven face. Far in the distance but really next to my ear, only sounding a million miles away, came the call of the lesser yellowlegs so faintly. *Pill-e-wee.* Almost a wild whisper in my ear. *Pill-e-wee . . . pill-a-wee.* Come home, John, come home, all is well, you are welcome.

"It's making a little sound!" It was the woman who spoke again.

"That's a wild sound; do not forget that sound. Hope that you will always be able to hear that wild sound somewhere."

The woman's eyes moistened and she rubbed them but it did no good, for the tears began to flow again, and she cried openly for the wild thing she had never really noticed until a man came into her kitchen and told her a wild tale of flight and function. The boys were silent.

"You place a lot of importance on that little bird, don't you, mister."

"I guess I do; yes, I guess I do."

I held the bird between thumb and middle finger and squeezed until that thumb and finger met through the body, crushing ribs with a familiar cracking of small bones; I could feel the heart frantic pounding and still I crushed, until the banded lesser yellowlegs twitched a few times and struggled briefly but then lay limp in my hands.

"You killed it!"

"It was dead long before it came to this farm."

"We were trying to keep it alive!"

"Yellowlegs don't eat bread." I spread the feathers of the breast. "This animal's been shot; it's an old wound. It's been stuck in some kind of chemical; you can smell it on the wing. It's been chewed by a cat. It's been fed bread." I held out the limp body. "But it never belonged to any country club, never paid any taxes, never obeyed a speed limit other than its own, never read a no trespassing sign, never went to war, never obeyed the laws of any tyrant, never served on any very important committee and never ran for public office."

The man looked with interest.

"Thanks."

"You're welcome. That's why I've come."

"Anytime, mister, you come on back anytime, give us a biology lesson."

"Need to get rid of these goddamn cats. I'm not sure it was ever intended for man to keep cats."

I kicked the Mercury into life, punched in the cassette with the five-string banjo exploding inside, spilling out over the Kansas pasture and plowed fields for hundreds of yards, and threw the bird on the seat. The pedal jammed into the rubber floormat, spitting gravel up into fender wells and out over the driveway, clattering against a wooden shed, sending cats scurrying, wrenching the wheel; and still with the pedal jammed, I turned north back home, back home with a dead banded yellowlegs lying on a front car seat.

It had all become so clear now, why I was here and what a task I had set about without really knowing it. Perspective, though, my year's research had added some perspective, as well as levels of commitment that might not have been there before, and had forced me to put ideas together, large ideas that unified my environment in a way no other kind of experience could. View the planet as an Ultimate Machine in need of a Master Mechanic's touch, as a set of interconnected working parts, that's what one had to do, view the planet as a set of interconnected parts in which the functions of even the smallest, most seemingly insignificant part depended upon the smooth function of all others, in this set of rules and stimuli and responses and structures reactions and actions, so vast and complicated that it cannot be understood so must be felt. One could never completely understand so complex an Ultimate Machine. There was no "Master Mechanic" for Earth, but there *was* the unique touch of the Master Mechanic, which derived mostly from the deepest romantic appreciation for all parts, I concluded, speeding now, faster, faster, fence posts, bar ditches, telephone poles, gravel driveways, asphalt ribbon highway, signs, worn painted stripes, green wheat blowing in shallow waves across miles and miles and miles as far as the eye could see, out on the plains I love and to the horizon I always have to have there. To know the part was there, even to be willing to acknowledge the part was there when introduced, no matter whether one understood its function—*that* was the requirement for driving a second-hand Merc or a second-hand Planet. And if one didn't *know* the part was there or how it might be essential, one still assumed that there might be more to the machine than could immediately be seen. And if there was more, then the "more" might well have some basic reason for being there. That kind of faith in unknown workings went well beyond the classic and into the romantic, and although the classic could delude on a grand scale, and while the romantic might never command any one thing at any one time, the romantic could nevertheless provide the eternal framework upon which to hang and arrange the thoughts which would guarantee the survivals of species. "Eternal" up to physical limits, of course. The sun would fade away into a dull red thing with enough time, but when that day arrived, even the yellowlegs might well be ready for it, deciding long before that enough trips to Argentina had been taken. In the meantime, I had a charge: take that sense of the Master Mechanic, a sense that I in truth did not possess in great amounts, apply it to a world in which I lived, then teach it (= fix?) to the world as a value set for wild things. Sounded so simple.

The river appeared then and I slowed, turning off into the gravel place where generations of fishermen had parked to try their luck, but I did not silence the engine. Instead, I pried the band from the leg of a dead bird on the seat and removed it from the drying leg. Once removed, I pressed it again into a ring. The body I threw from the window as far as I could and watched it sail out over some

191

cottonwoods to land on the sand. The worn part had been returned to its proper place. Ants and other insects could convert the body back to carbon and nitrogen, and eventually that carbon and nitrogen might find its way back into the body of a yellowlegs, even possibly, I thought, into a descendant of this very bird. I took a piece of twine from my field bag and strung it through the band. I had to go back now, go back and teach some biology lessons and tell of the value of some experiences and attitudes I'd learned along the way.

I tied the string around my neck and the worn band hung down as a necklace inside my shirt. I pulled it out and read the band number at last. It was not a familiar number, but it spoke in its own way of an unknown person who had come close to a part of nature not everyone knew existed. I never returned the band; I felt even then it was mine to keep. And as I put my second-hand Merc into gear and headed back north out across the face of my second-hand planet, I felt then an obligation I was not sure any other man had.

So that's the end of my tale of a year spent studying the natural history of *Tringa flavipes* (Gmelin) 1789, the lesser yellowlegs. Classes begin tomorrow, and I will walk into that auditorium at eight-thirty in the morning to face a sea of anxious freshmen. They are all, each and every one of them, citizens of the realm, and they all, each and every one of them, some day in their futures will make decisions that will help turn this Ultimate Machine I call Earth. They will all expect the world from me, beginning tomorrow morning, and tomorrow they will damn well get it! You ask "why?" and of course I can answer that question without hesitation: I have returned, I have seen the yellowlegs in the wilderness, I have set down my thoughts of that vision, and I have followed that banded gray lady to the end. That's why.

192